Alien Americans

A STUDY OF RACE RELATIONS

BY B. SCHRIEKE

New York

THE VIKING PRESS

1936

FIRST PUBLISHED MARCH 1936

". . . one Nation, indivisible, with Liberty and Justice for all."

"I do not plead for black more than I plead for white education. The South cannot rise unless the Negro rises. Nor can the Negro rise unless the white man is educated too. So long as the Negro is down, the white man will stay down. . . . Eight million ignorant Negroes must be an eternal drag on their white neighbors, and these neighbors, if ignorant, will not permit the Negro to prosper unless they too are educated and prosper."
—JOHN GRAHAM BROOKS, *An American Citizen: The Life of William Henry Baldwin, Jr.*

"I am interested in the Negro because I am interested in America."
—JULIUS ROSENWALD

"E Pluribus Unum."

Introduction

In 1933, while I was still in Java, the Board of Trustees of the Julius Rosenwald Fund invited me to come to this country in order to make a study of Negro life and education, especially in the Southern states, on the basis of my extensive but quite different experience with education and race relations in the Orient.

Although fully realizing the difficulties involved in this assignment, I gladly accepted the invitation. After being graduated at the University of Leiden as a doctor of Oriental philology, and after spending nearly eighteen years in the Dutch East Indies as an officer in the Bureau of Native Affairs, as Assistant Commissioner of Native Affairs, as Director of the Museum in Batavia, as Professor of Social Anthropology and Sociology at the University of Batavia, and finally as Secretary of Education and Religious Worship for the Dutch East Indies, I felt that a stay in the United States would be highly instructive to me.

Although the problems the Board wished me to study were entirely foreign to me, since I had never visited the United States nor had I ever met an American Negro, the Board regarded these handicaps as an advantage, as a guarantee of unbiased opinion.

Before leaving for the United States I visited the libraries of the International Labour Office and of the League of Nations in Geneva, and the Bibliothèque de Documentation Internationale Contemporaine in Paris, in order to get some acquaintance with the subject.

On September 15, 1934, I arrived in New York and at once proceeded to Chicago, where I spent a few weeks in reading and adapting myself to the language, people, manners, and customs. It was necessary for me not only to study the Negro situation, but, in order to understand as fully as possible the peculiar character of these problems, also to become familiar with the American background and the American reaction to bi-racial situations other than Negro-white.

My study was confined to the continental United States. The Hawaiian Islands, American Samoa, the Philippine Islands, Guam, Alaska, the Virgin Islands, and Puerto Rico are excluded from this survey.

The months from October 1934 until May 1935 were employed in travel and observation. I spent most of my time in the cities of New York, Washington, and Boston, and in the states of Virginia, North Carolina, Georgia, Tennessee, Arkansas, Louisiana, Oklahoma, New Mexico, and California. Visits—some of them extending over several days—were paid to Bay St. Louis and Jackson in Mississippi; Tuskegee, Alabama; Charleston, South Carolina; parts of Arizona; and to Harvard and Yale Universities. Everywhere I found the kindest reception and hospitality. Everyone was eager to give me the information I wanted and to bring me in touch with those who were regarded as the best authorities on the subject.

On the first of May I was back in Chicago, and spent the period until September writing this report. I have based my conclusions upon personal observation, upon conversations with persons intimately connected with the problems studied, and upon wide reading of authoritative literature in the field in order to check the accuracy of my impressions and to avoid mistakes or misrepresentations. I have refrained, however, from the use of footnotes referring to the literature: for the scholar they seem superfluous; for the general reader they are only tiresome and distracting. The literature mentioned at the end of the book is not an exhaustive bibliography, but is simply a testimony of gratitude on my part to those authors to whom I feel most indebted for the understanding of the problems which are touched upon in this report.

In concluding this introduction, I want to thank the Board of Trustees of the Julius Rosenwald Fund for the great opportunity it has given to me and for the independence and freedom it has allowed me in forming my impressions and expressing them.

—B. SCHRIEKE

Chicago, Illinois
September 1, 1935

Contents

Alien Americans

CHAPTER I

The Chinese in California

CALIFORNIA was ceded to the United States by Mexico on February 2, 1848, by the treaty of Guadalupe Hidalgo. Gold had been discovered in California during the preceding month, but it was not until autumn that the news became generally known. The gold craze swept from the United States to all corners of the globe. Drawn by the lure of the precious metal, men hastened towards California: rowdy adventurers, speculators of every class and nationality—a restless, lawless, reckless crowd of men, jealous and greedy, determined to make no less than a fortune as easily and as quickly as possible. They had left behind all claims to social recognition based on family, social ties, or previous attainments. In the rough life of the early California mining camp, distinction was commanded solely by vigour and personal courage. It is estimated that by the summer of 1849 there were at least 20,000 men at work in the diggings and that 77,000 persons entered California in 1849; 82,000, in 1850.

Among the first to go to the mining districts were many American soldiers who had served in the Mexican War. Naturally, they did not take too kindly to the presence in the camps of Spaniards and Mexicans, many of whom were skilled miners able to locate the more valuable claims and to work them to better advantage. Their "greasy," "swarthy" appearance inspired disgust. As the Americans, who had been in the minority, increased in numbers, they began, with the cry of

3

"California for Americans!" forcibly to eject the despised
dark-skinned and under-sized foreigners from Mexico, South
America, and southern Europe (including the French) "who
were stealing the gold of the United States." English, German, and Irish miners helped the native Americans. Blood
flowed abundantly, and anarchy reigned in the camps. Finally
the foreigners were compelled to abandon their claims. Many
moved to the cities or to the southern districts; thousands returned to their native lands rather than submit to indignities
and persecution; and others became robbers and bandits. The
agitation against the dark-skinned foreigners spread to San
Francisco.

The anti-foreign feeling in California was unquestionably
intensified by the presence of Southerners, who comprised
nearly one-third of her population in the first decade of American rule. Of these a minority were of educated, pure American
stock. In some cases they brought with them their slaves and
a profound conviction that California should be a white man's
country. But this class was greatly outnumbered by immigrants
from the border states, whose ignorance and extreme race
antipathies classed together all persons other than white Europeans.

To that feeling contributed also the hatred against the Indian, now especially intense because of the attacks of the plains
Indians upon whites passing through their country while
crossing the continent to California. The Christianized, virtually enslaved Mission Indian of California was of a degraded
type and aroused only contempt on the part of the settlers
and newcomers.

"Poor whites" of the frontier of Georgia had been the first
to draw the colour line against the Indian. In 1774, therefore,
the government of Georgia had ordained that the murder of
an Indian should be punishable under the laws of the province

even as was the murder of a white man. The preamble to this law observed that the law was passed because "it has been represented that some Indians in amity with this province have been barbarously murdered, to the great scandal of society and the danger of involving the province in a bloody and expensive war; and there is reason to believe that several ill-disposed persons have not considered such inhuman actions in a proper light but being influenced by the ill-grounded prejudice which ignorant minds are apt to conceive against persons differing in colour from themselves, and, unaware of the consequences, have looked on these murders rather as meritorious. . . ."

Before this time, during the French and Indian War (1754–63), Virginia had offered scalp bounties [1] as an incentive for soldiers and farmers to kill Indians siding with the French. Eager for scalp money, German settlers in the mountains—part ancestors of the "mountain whites" in the Appalachians today—led by a British officer, ambushed and slew forty Cherokees, who had entered the war on the English side. Of course the bounty was given for any Indian scalp as the hair of a French Indian could not be distinguished from that of an English one. In December 1763 a group of Presbyterian Scotch-Irish frontiersmen, "in private life, virtuous and respectable, not cruel but mild and merciful," collected in this way bounties offered by Pennsylvania—in its proclamation of war against the Delaware Indians (1756)—for the scalps of Indian converts of Moravian missionaries living in three tiny

---

[1] This method was introduced in 1641 by Wilhelmus Kieft, Dutch director-general of New Netherland—presumably imitating a similar practice in the East Indies—and later on was adopted by the Puritans. It was, in a way, a money-saving expedient. If the frontier farmers could be encouraged to make offensive war against the Indians on a commission basis, fewer regular soldiers —paid and maintained by the government during long periods of inactivity— would be needed. The last American scalp bounty was offered by the Territory of Indiana in 1814 as an "encouragement to the enterprise and bravery of our fellow citizens."

settlements in north-eastern Pennsylvania. Did not "the Scripture command that the heathen should be destroyed"? The Reverend Mr. Elder, pastor of these murderers, condoned their act and failed to assist the authorities in their apprehension and punishment, warning that it was "dangerous to act in opposition to an outraged multitude." In fact, the murders were generally and popularly approved. General Samuel Curtis—in his report on the Sand Creek massacre in Colorado (1864), for which the Methodist preacher and ex-missionary to the Indians, the Reverend Mr. Chivington, was responsible—stated that the popular cry of settlers and soldiers on the frontier favoured an indiscriminate slaughter which was very difficult to restrain. He wrote: "I abhor this style, but so it goes, from Minnesota to Texas. . . ."

John Beeson, one of the early emigrants to Oregon—not a sentimental humanitarian, but a hard-headed, practical man of affairs—publishing his notes in the decade before the Civil War, writes about the covered-wagon epoch: "The majority of the first emigration to Oregon were from Missouri; and among them it was customary to speak of the Indian man as a buck; of the woman as a squaw; until, at length, in the general acceptance of the terms, they ceased to recognize the rights of humanity in those to whom they were so applied. By a very natural and easy transition, from being spoken of as brutes, they came to be thought of as game to be shot, or as vermin to be destroyed." In another passage Beeson gives us a picture of the sentiment of that period: "On another occasion, a white man being found dead, he was supposed to have been killed by Indians. A company was made up forthwith, an Indian ranch was surrounded, and all the inmates put to death, men, women, and children. The domineering spirit grew by what it fed on, until, excited to madness by these oft-recurring scenes of blood, men became utterly regardless of justice, even towards those of their own race. Whatever a man's private views might be, he was expected to go with the crowd, to the full extent of every enterprise. . . . Personal freedom was thus frequently invaded; and life itself was not secure."

In Oregon the legislature, the subordinate Indian agents, the Methodist clergy, and the Know-Nothing political party—all were directly implicated in systematically carrying on "Indian wars." The destruction of the Indians was advocated openly. During this period of agitation a slump in the mining industry left many miners unemployed. These unemployed were supported for many months at good pay as soldiers of the state, their only duties being to go out in bodies and kill Indians—women, "the very seeds of increase," and children included.

In California the extermination of the Indians began in 1849 and continued until well on into the seventies. One of the early settlers wrote concerning events in which he participated at the late date of August 15, 1865: "I had often argued with Good regarding the disposition of the Indians. He believed in killing every man or well-grown boy, but in leaving the women unmolested in their mountain retreats. It was plain to me that we must also get rid of the women." Another settler wrote of an occurrence in April 1871: "The next day the whites trail the Indians with dogs, corner them in a cave, and kill about thirty. In the cave with the men were some Indian children. Kingsley could not bear to kill children with his fifty-six caliber rifle. 'It tore them up so bad.' So he did it with his thirty-eight caliber Smith and Wesson revolver." Such were the feelings of many of the early whites on the Pacific Coast. In California, without the ratification of any treaty or the semblance of purchase, the native Indians were completely dispossessed—in so far as the white man wished—during the first half-century of United States possession.

All these circumstances helped to establish the antagonism against the "dark-skinned foreigners." The repulsive stereotype had become "set" in definite feeling and emotional pattern.

It was during the gold-rush period that, enticed by the "Golden Romance," the first Chinese arrived in California. As soon as they began to enter the placer regions in ever-increasing numbers, the anti-foreign feeling of the whites, at first directed against the Spanish-Americans, was turned also against the Chinese. Their physical appearance, their queues, their strange attire, their habits of living, marked them as objects for attack. Their lack of political influence encouraged brutal treatment. This hostile attitude manifested itself in riots and attempted lynchings. During the fifties, through the efforts of the miners, the California state legislature passed several discriminatory laws intended to restrict immigration by taxation. Later, these laws were declared to be unconstitutional. Many Chinese left the mines, and the others confined themselves to the poorer or to the abandoned claims. Later on, when the mining corporations were organized, many of them were employed as labourers. In 1860, 60 per cent of the Chinese were in eleven mining counties engaged in mining and in domestic occupations. By 1870, only 45 per cent remained in these counties, while 38 per cent were now settled in and about the cities of San Jose, Sacramento, and San Francisco.

Driven from the mines, the Chinese had found employment as common labourers; as domestics; in the manufacture of cigars, boots, shoes, woollen goods, clothing, bags, oakum, soap, and candles. They worked as store-keepers, hotel-keepers, laundrymen, carpenters, cabinet-makers, upholsterers, carvers, restaurant cooks, and so on. They were to be found in lumber, paper, and powder mills, in tanneries, rope-walks, lead-works, and tin shops. There was scarcely a trade in which they did not engage.

In the beginning (1851–59) there was a labour vacuum. The fortune-seekers had no intention of performing menial, petty, and laborious tasks, or of earning their money as common labourers. Under these circumstances it can easily be understood how the Chinese got their chance. During this first period of western manufacturing, before organized white labour succeeded in gradually displacing the Chinese, many industries were monopolized by the latter. The making of boots, shoes, slippers, brooms, and underwear, the packing of pork and the drying of fish, were wholly in Chinese hands. The making of cigars, shirts, tinware, tallow, and jute products was almost entirely so. By 1865, 80 per cent of all the labour in the woollen mills of California was Chinese.

Several hundred Chinese were engaged in the fishing industry; thousands of them were employed in the canneries as year-round employees, seasonal labourers, and as emergency or extra labourers. The willingness of the Chinese to undertake any sort of labour was of particular value in a population largely made up of males. The lack of white female labour made the Chinese indispensable for work in the kitchen, in hotels and restaurants, in laundries, and in other activities.

But there was also plenty of work in other fields. Without Chinese labour the building of the Union Pacific, Northern Pacific, and Southern Pacific railroads would hardly have been possible. The delta region of the Sacramento Valley was a marshland. The wilderness had to be cleared.

The Chinese were needed, thousands of them. Poverty, famine, and ruin in China after the great Taiping rebellion (1850–64) made thousands emigrate from the agricultural districts of Kwang Tung to the "Golden Mountains." They reclaimed swamplands, constructed railroads, built levees and roads, graded and ditched land, and planted orchards and asparagus fields under the direction of a few white men who laid claim to thousands of acres of this new prosperous area. In 1870, 90 per cent of the agricultural labour of California was Chinese, and in 1880, nearly 75 per cent.

In the beginning, race prejudice was subordinated to industrial necessity. The Chinese were among "the most worthy of our newly adopted citizens," "our most orderly and industrious citizens," "the best immigrants in California"; they were "thrifty," "sober," "tractable," "inoffensive," "law-abiding"; they showed "an all-round ability" and an "adaptability" beyond praise. As labourers on the ranches they were not competitors, as they had been in the mines.

But in the cities, as years passed, as the immigration of whites continued and mining became less profitable, the manifold activities of the Chinese brought them again into competition with white labour in an increasingly large number of occupations. It was here that they became the bugaboo of the workingman and the politician. When the speculation bubble burst and the gold-hunters were driven to common tasks, they resented their situation and constituted an exceptionally unstable, discontented, and hostile labouring class.

The first agitation was organized against the Chinese cigarmakers (1859) but failed to accomplish anything of note. In 1866 one-half of the total number of proprietors of cigar factories in San Francisco were Chinese; 2000 of them were employed in the cigar-making trade, while only 200 whites were so engaged. By 1870 the number of Chinese cigar-makers had increased to 2800.

In February 1867 the white boot- and shoe-makers of San Francisco struck against a reduction in wages caused chiefly by the competition of Chinese labourers. The result was a race riot. The arrest, conviction, and sentencing of eleven men for participation therein aroused the white workers to a high pitch of excitement. Anti-coolie clubs were formed, later on organized as the Pacific Coast Anti-Coolie Association. In April another strike was lost. The boot and shoe manufacturers had a serious struggle for existence because of the competition of eastern factories and because of the high wage-rates demanded by the California workers. Chinese labourers had early been employed in the trade, and as years passed and additional demands for still higher wages were made upon the employers, employment of Chinese seemed the only solution to the problem. Opposition to their employment gradually became more bitter and determined. Before the close of the sixties the agitation against them, led by the boot- and shoe-makers' union, had grown to threatening proportions, and in the later seventies it came to a most startling climax.

During the elections of 1867, as in many subsequent campaigns, the bitterness of colour prejudice was evoked to win the restless workingmen. For the first time in the history of the state the two chief political parties pledged themselves to enact legislation which would protect Californians from Mongolian competition.

The Chinese were now "a distinct people," "unassimilable," "keeping to their own customs and laws." They "did not settle in America"; they "carried back gold to their homes"; they "went back to China." Their mere presence "lowered the plane of living"; they "shut out the white labour." They were "clannish," "dangerous" because of their secret societies, "criminal," "secretive in their actions," "debased and servile," "deceitful and vicious," "inferior from a mental and moral point of view, immeasurably lower than the Indians, for instance." They "smuggled opium" and "spread the use of it," and their Chinatowns were "full of prostitution and gambling." They were "filthy and loathsome in their habits," and their "unsanitary quarters made the neighbourhood uninhabitable." They were "undesirable as workers and as residents of the country." This was not merely an expression of opinion but a form of propaganda intended to create an attitude of hostility. Every aspect of the invaders became obnoxious and irritating. Their yellow skin was unpleasant; their slant eyes bespoke slyness; their conversation among themselves was frightful jabbering.

It has been stated above how the Chinese became the focus of the existing prejudice against foreigners. The fact that they took up whatever work the white man scorned bred contempt. Moreover, they were called "coolies," a term which means merely "unskilled labourer," but which for the American conveys the odious idea of semi-slavery. Apart from this there was another emotional association with Chinese labour that enraged the white workingman. The agitation against the Chinese not only coincided but also was combined with the campaign against the competition of convict labour (the sale of convict labour goods).

The change in the attitude of the white population was brought about by the completion of the Central Pacific railroad (1864–69), which filled San Francisco with unskilled labour and at the same time broke the isolation of the West so far as competition with the industries of the East and the immigration of white labour from the East in search for work on the Pacific Coast were concerned. Besides, the time of feverish prosperity and great speculative activity immediately after the Civil War had been followed by a reaction. The yield of the gold mines had declined steadily after 1865. Business stagnated. The unemployed crowded into the cities. Two successive years of drought (1869–71) lessened the demand for agricultural labour. There was a panic in the silver stocks (1872).

The concurrence of all these circumstances, which caused a

serious depression (1869–73), made inevitable a readjustment of occupations and wages. The ratification of the Burlingame treaty between the United States and China (1869), which for the sake of the railroads encouraged Chinese immigration, incensed organized and unorganized white labour, which relentlessly opposed the Chinese. In 1869 the presence in San Francisco [2] of thousands of Chinese, many of them recently discharged by the Central Pacific railroad, coupled with conditions resulting from business depression, aroused the incessant antagonism of the unemployed. A peculiarly virulent epidemic of smallpox was attributed to the Chinese. In April 1870 this agitation took on a violent aspect. It was caused in part by an announcement of the Southern Pacific railroad that it intended to use Chinese labour on its projected construction work, and in part by the arrival of 1300 fresh "Chinks," [3] at a time when economic conditions were most unsatisfactory. Parades, mass meetings, conventions, and boycotts were organized by the unions, led by the shoe-makers. Pamphlets and circulars by the thousands were printed and distributed. Petitions were sent to the state legislature, and to the President of the United States and the Senate, praying for relief from the encroachments of the Chinese.

At the end of 1872 nearly one-half of the workingmen employed in the factories of San Francisco were Chinese. In 1873, 17,000 new Chinese immigrants arrived. The flow of cheap labour became overwhelming. The continued decline in ore production and in dividends caused two more severe panics in mining stocks (1872, 1875). Banks closed their doors. The collapse was terrifying. The seriousness of the situation was

[2] The population of San Francisco was about 460 in August 1847; 21,802 in 1850 (20,439 males); 146,528 in 1860 (116,934 males); 209,831 in 1870 (150,058 males); 292,874 in 1880 (208,526 males).

[3] The numbers of the Chinese had increased from 25,000 at the end of 1852, and 35,000 in 1860, to 65,763 in 1868.

aggravated by the increasing stream of immigrants from the East, who tried to escape the depression there.[4]

In January 1876 a new crash came. Business houses failed, banks and mines closed, agriculture suffered from want of rain and capital. California faced its most serious industrial and financial crisis. Nevertheless, more than 22,000 new Chinese immigrants entered the state. The attitude of the 15,000 unemployed whites in the city of San Francisco became threatening. Crimes of all kinds increased in numbers. Crowds of desperate men unleashed their pent-up wrath on the despised hordes of Chinese, "the moon-eyed lepers" who had brought low wages, unemployment, and hunger to the white labourer. The cry, "The Chinese must go!" became the rallying slogan for the masses. Demonstrations resulted in riots, bloodshed, pillage, and incendiarism (1876–78). The civil authorities, wishing to show the voters that they were "with the people" and opposed to the corporations, pandered to the mob and were lax in controlling the situation. Several anti-Chinese laws and ordinances were enacted, but the demand for complete exclusion became overwhelming. Resolutions and petitions to that end, asking relief from the serious menace of the Chinese, were passed in rapid succession. The employers also joined the movement as the Chinese began to establish their own shops, to hire their own countrymen, and to enter into direct competition with their former instructors. Moreover, the Chinese also had learned to strike. Capital—thus threatened and somewhat frightened by the white workers, who, organized in the Workingmen's Party, had succeeded in electing their candidates as mayors, assemblymen, and senators and in taking an active and prominent part in the drafting and adoption of a new state constitution (1878–79)—allied with labour in the

[4] In the period 1873–75 more than 154,000 persons arrived in California from the East.

struggle against the Chinese. In 1876 both of the national political parties already had inserted anti-Chinese planks in their platforms. On September 3, 1879, a state-wide vote on the advisability of complete exclusion recorded the decision of 154,638 citizens for exclusion and 883 against it. "John Chinaman" had to go!

Although in 1882 and again in 1892 the immigration from China was formally suspended, it lasted until 1902, when Congress extended indefinitely all laws relating to Chinese exclusion. Meanwhile their numbers had increased to 107,500 in 1890, partly as a result of illegal entry. The Act of 1892 excluded 30,000 who were legally domiciled here. The murder of Chinese and the destruction of Chinese property, especially during the orgy of 1885 in the Northwest after the completion of the Northern Pacific (1883) and Canadian Pacific railroads, drove others out. Those who decided to remain in this country were refused the right of naturalization. For this they did not care so much; the majority had not come with the idea of making their homes in this country and had no specific desire to become American citizens. Their life here was influenced very little by the customs and institutions of the New World. There were enough of them to allow them to form their own communities. They retained their own habits of eating and dress, and their own institutions, and they were able to get along without learning English. In this way they segregated themselves and were segregated.

Since 1890 the number of Chinese in the continental United States has declined:

1890	107,500	
1900	90,000	(9,000 American-born)
1910	71,500	(15,000 American-born)
1920	61,639	(18,532 American-born)
1930	74,954	(30,868 American-born)

After 1920 the number of foreign-born Chinese remained practically unchanged: 43,107 in 1920; 44,086 in 1930. On the other hand, unless the figures of 1920 are an underestimate, there has been a considerable increase in the American-born group: 18,532 in 1920; 30,868 in 1930. The distribution of the sexes is still disproportionate: of the total Chinese population of 74,954 in 1930 there were 59,802 males and 15,152 females. Since 1920 the number of Chinese in California has increased from 28,812 to 37,261 in 1930. This increase has gone to San Francisco: 7744 in 1920; 16,303 in 1930. The Chinese in San Francisco now represent 22 per cent of the total Chinese population of the United States, and 44 per cent of the Chinese population in California.

In the decade between 1882 and 1892 the agitation against the Chinese was carried on intermittently, but from 1892 to the Immigration Act of 1924, by which Orientals were barred from immigration to this country, anti-Chinese feeling gradually declined. Between 1901 and 1924 it was noticeable only in so far as the Chinese were included in the anti-Japanese agitation. After 1924 organized opposition died away. The remaining Chinese scattered over different states, moved into the towns, tended to take on American ways and higher standards of living, or drifted into non-competitive or less productive urban occupations. Relations of accommodation became established, and the Chinese question lost its economic importance.

In the California papers, news about tong wars, gambling houses, and traffic in narcotics still keeps alive the traditional opinion about the Chinese inclination to crime. Gambling dens, however, are regarded as an inevitable concomitant of Chinese life and are seldom disturbed. Although sanitary conditions in Chinatown are still far from ideal, the Chinese is no longer characteristically dirty and no longer spreads disease. Tolerant indifference to the Chinese has taken the place of hatred on the part of the Americans. It is admitted that many Chinese are worthy, interesting, and exceedingly honest people. The typical picture of the modern American Chinese shows him as keeping his undesirable characteristics largely to himself, staying in his place, and being harmless and even valuable. However, his social status is fixed; there is a recognized and established social distance. He is still mysterious and unknown, but this makes him romantic, as he is no longer feared. Ladies do not mind going shopping all by themselves in the Chinese quarter. Dining in a Chinese restaurant is a form of recreation, and picturesque Chinatown stirs the imagination.

On the other hand, like the Jews who see the modern Ghetto as a menace to their status as persons and as citizens, the educated Chinese think that Chinatown is a disgrace to the race. They resent it since Americans are apt to judge the Chinese by Chinatown and its occupants. For the same reason they resent derogatory pictures of their race and its characterization in popular literature and movies. Folk terms such as "Chinaman" or "Chink" sting their race consciousness. The discrimination they encounter often develops in them a kind of oppression psychosis which manifests itself in an excessive sensitivity. As a result of this they are prone to attribute all unpleasant experiences, even their own failures, to discrimination. They identify their personal status with that of their race. As with other minority groups, there is a complete incapacity to view their own problems objectively. Oppression psychosis implies the tendency to personal interpretation. There is always a chip on the shoulder to which the slightest jar calls attention. This sometimes leads, through a process of compensation, to race pride and an exalted conception of themselves; but whatever the individual reaction to their personal experiences may be, the human desire for recognition and the rebuffs administered by American society force them back to their own communities unless they have the courage to fight single-handed. Nevertheless, the faith of American-born Chinese in the ideal qualities of American institutions is unshaken. Their only resentment is due to the fact that these ideals are practically unattainable by them because of their race.

Chinese are—as a rule—not debarred from the white hotels and restaurants, but they are denied the use of many swimming pools, gymnasiums, tennis courts, and golf courses. Some barber shops and some "high-tone" stores will not give them service, and it is very difficult for them to find homes in the better districts of the cities. The social clubs and other organizations often exclude them from their circles, sometimes openly, sometimes just by making them feel uncomfortable. Therefore, as a precaution against embarrassment, they do not want to go anywhere unless they are sure that no restrictions will be imposed. They are being forced to stay together as a group separated from the American community. As a result of the rebuffs they have experienced, they have become more cautious, even suspicious, in their dealings with white Americans. They have learned the wisdom of keeping their thoughts to themselves and, consequently, seem cold and expressionless. This attitude on their part confirms the white American in his opinion about their racial characteristics: their secretiveness, their cunning, their incomprehensible ways, and their inassimilability. Nevertheless, their contacts with their white fellow-citizens are more frequent than with their co-Asiatics (the Japanese).

The school, the place where the American-born Chinese have their contacts with American life and where they acquire the Occidental culture, has played a great role in this process of accommodation. At the same time, however, it has introduced a wide chasm between the older and younger generations in the Chinese homes. The majority of the American-born Chinese tend to drift away from their parents and their Asiatic heritage, being eager to follow the pattern set by the "American" family, as they see it. The greatest difficulty is that the two generations represent divergent "universes of discourse." The younger generation with its different "apperception mass" cannot speak with its parents about problems which are rooted in a social world entirely foreign and irrelevant to the elders because of dissimiliarity of experience. Moreover, the children cannot explain them in Chinese. Another difficulty is the marriage problem. The parents are inclined to arrange the marriages, as is the custom in China, but the children object.

In a way this conflict between the two generations is quite natural. Always and everywhere in the world the opinion about the younger generation has been rather pessimistic. The *laudatores temporis acti* are a universal phenomenon. In Europe of the nineteenth and twentieth centuries—since the idea of progress captured many minds, and youth became more aggressive—this conflict, indicative of social change, has been accentuated. In America, as a result of the sweeping industrial revolution and the transformation of family life, it is still stronger. So long as such conflicts occur within the individual's traditional society, social restrictions prevent too great a shock; but in the immigrant family two cultural heritages, two sets of social standards, two behaviour patterns clash in the conflict of the generations. The children become Americanized, while the parents firmly hold to their native *mores* and traditions. The changing social-economic conditions in America (industrialization, urbanization, and their consequences), to which the American pattern of family life has not yet adapted itself, intensify the difficulty. In the case of the Asiatic immigrants the shock must be all the greater, for, according to the traditional standard of the patriarchal Asiatic family, the revolt of the children against parental authority is a horror, a sacrilege. On the other hand the segregation of the Chinese community by the outside American world forces the young Chinese to arrive at some kind of readjustment. This makes the position of the American-born Chinese more difficult, for he acts as a Chinese at home, and as an American while with Americans. In both cases he is likely to be criticized, and at the same time his personality is disorganized.

The school not only introduces the young Chinese into the American world but also—through contacts with their schoolmates—develops in them a racial consciousness that tends to make them withdraw from association with the Americans and associate only with their own group in school and outside. There is increasing tension from grammar school to college. The higher the institution, the more the Chinese feel excluded. The American universities usually classify the American-born Chinese as foreign students; they must go through the advisory office for foreign students. Such experiences inevitably lead to disillusionment, which makes many Chinese pass through a period of emotional disturbance that is generally solved by a return to the Chinese community and its restraining influences.

As a result of their American education, the American-born Chinese are becoming dissatisfied with their parents' social and economic status, which they are inclined to regard as the cause of the existing prejudice. Therefore, in order to become fused with the American group, they prepare themselves for some profession or skilled occupation which is respected by the Americans. Here again they meet obstacles. In American society the "Chinaman" has his recognized and established place, which he must keep, even though the shaky three-legged stool of chop suey, laundry, and fan tan can hardly be called a sound economic foundation. Again, the American-born Chinese feel discriminated against because of their race. On account of their physiognomy the average American reacts to them in the same way as to their parents, classifies them in the same group, and treats them as though they were aliens. Even though they prepare themselves for vocations where they might be on an equality with the white American citizens, business firms offer them no opportunity to practise what they learn at school, and the Chinese community has no use for them since it does not have big business establishments. For this reason they prefer the professions by means of which they will not be dependent on the whims of white employers. However, the professional field offers relatively few opportunities. The limited number of Chinese and their somewhat restricted wealth make it impossible to depend only on Chinese clients, while prejudice in American society and the competition of white colleagues prohibit a general and lucrative practice. Because of the colour line, the teaching profession is practically closed to them. Indeed, the vocational entrance into the American group is very narrow. The steadily growing number of American-born Chinese with higher education makes the problem increasingly difficult.

If the American-born Chinese go to China—as some have done, hoping to find a position there—language, life, and society are foreign to them, and they are not accepted as fellow-countrymen. Unless the American-born Chinese are willing to struggle for their opportunities by competing with Americans—ready to take rebuffs rather than to accept inferior status, hoping that they will be employed on the basis of merit and that prejudice gradually will disappear—they must seek status in the Chinese community; otherwise they will fall into an attitude of hopelessness. And disillusionment results in an inferiority complex. On the other hand the struggle for status in this country on the part of the American-born is not encouraged by the older generation, however much they would like their children to get ahead. They fear the revival of the painful experiences of the latter part of the nineteenth century which no old Chinese has forgotten. What they dread most is a return of that feeling of hatred which would disturb the existing stability in social relationships.

Meanwhile, it will be very interesting to observe the great change that will take place when Chinatown in Los Angeles disappears. This area is needed for the construction of the new Union Station. The city intends to build a new Chinatown, but the Chinese population is not willing to move there. The displacement of the Chinese already has taken another direction. Dissatisfied with the physical and social conditions in the traditional neighbourhood, many of them have already moved out to the district east of San Pedro and west of Central Avenue between Ninth and Thirty-Sixth Streets, where they live among Japanese, Mexicans, Jews, Negroes, and eastern Europeans. If this movement continues in Los Angeles and spreads to other cities, it may lead to a break in the isolation of the Chinese. Finally, through fusion and intermixture with the other underprivileged nationalities, as the older generation passes away with the years, it may lead to a brighter future.

CHAPTER II

The Japanese in California

THE gap in the labour supply caused by the exclusion of the Chinese in the eighties and nineties was filled by the Japanese. Over a half-million acres of farmland had been put out of cultivation. From Bakersfield to Redding, banks had mortgages on farmlands that could not be made productive. No wonder the Japanese were welcomed by the public press! The large land-owners of California who had been deprived of their farmhands found, in the Japanese, excellent workers for their farms and orchards, workers who were willing to do the meanest tasks at lower wages than the Chinese. The central portion of the San Joaquin Valley represents the heart of the oldest Japanese farming district in California. Here the Japanese were the pioneers who reclaimed the land from the desert and blazed the trail for the horde of other nationalities that followed. The Imperial Valley was turned by the Japanese from its unhealthy barren state of wasteland into the richest and most productive district in the state of California.

Almost all of the Japanese immigrants came from the rural districts of Japan, the majority from the Hiroshima, Kumamoto, Wakayama, Okayama, Fukuoka, and Yamaguchi *kens* (prefectures). Consequently, most of them were of the peasant type. In the early days the Japanese started as drifting transient labourers; but after some years of "following the seasons" they saved enough money to return to Japan and marry, or else to marry by the "picture-bride" method. Then they reclaimed land, or purchased it, and built up farms.

Emigration from Japan and Hawaii was encouraged through advertising by steamship companies and by labour contractors. The inducements offered to the Japanese began to have perceptible effect in 1891, when their arrivals numbered 1136; there were 2844 in 1899 and 12,626 in 1900. According to volume 15 of the *Report of the United States Industrial Commission,* there was in 1900 in the state of California alone "a great army of Japanese coolies, numbering upwards of 20,-000," which had already secured a monopoly of the labour in the agricultural industries.

From 1898 to 1907 there was a new period of prosperity in the United States. The railroad system of the West was not yet completed, and the demand for cheap labour continued. So more Japanese labour was imported under contract.

The opposition against the Japanese developed soon after they began to arrive in great numbers. The farm-owners found that the Japanese were not so easily controlled as the Chinese had been: they had all the vices of the latter and none of the virtues. Where the Chinese were docile, the Japanese were aggressive. They demanded better employment and housing conditions, violated contracts, struck when the strike would be most inopportune for the farmer, and were eager to become land-owners. Farmers frequently were forced to lease or sell their ranches to the Japanese because the latter, having a monopoly on the farm labour in the community, employed that monopoly most effectively in bringing financial loss to farmers who resisted their demands. Soon the Japanese were virtually in control of the berry, potato, flower, and truck-garden markets in almost every community of any size. Another complaint was that they neglected the orchards and teams furnished them, and that the farms leased to them were permitted to deteriorate rapidly. In thinning vegetables, a process in which wages were paid by the thousand feet, they worked less carefully than the Mexicans in order to increase their earnings. If for that reason Mexican labour was preferred, the Japanese stirred up the Mexicans to work with as little care as they themselves did. Although the organization of Japanese labour under bosses was very convenient for the small rancher whose need for men varied greatly from week to week, this organization made the rancher entirely dependent on the bosses, who abused their power in many cases.

In the cities the Japanese became small merchants, restaurant proprietors, laundrymen, domestics, and gardeners. They worked on railway section gangs and in mines and canneries. They were accused of maintaining sweat shops, of driving white female domestics out of employment, of forcing two hundred shoe-repair men away from San Francisco, of controlling all unskilled labour on the railroads, of cutting into the white laundry business, and of underbidding white building contractors from 20 to 26 per cent. In fact they did cut prices and wages, and thus aroused the antagonism of the merchant and working classes. The Japanese refused to remain in a special quarter of their own and were willing to pay excessively high prices or rentals for pieces of property in other sections. When they moved in, white families in the adjoining properties moved out; and the neighbourhood, invaded by persons against whom public opinion had turned, lost status. Property values were reduced, and the Japanese were frequently enabled to buy or rent buildings and residences on their own terms. These practices aroused the white landlords, who by various means attempted to prevent the Japanese from spreading into all parts of a city.

Part of this awakening anti-Japanese opinion was contributed, of course, by the already existing unfavourable stereotype of the Oriental and by the slumbering anti-Oriental tradition of the Coast—the element dormant in its *mores* and impressed on it by the antecedent Chinese experiences. This complex had only to be aroused by similar emotional associations or stimuli in order to become active again and to produce the same reactions and attitudes.

The Western Central Labor Union in Seattle started the anti-Japanese movement (April 18, 1900). In California the first gun was fired, in San Francisco, when, on May 7, 1900, Dr. A. E. Ross at a meeting of the State and San Francisco Building Trades Councils criticized unrestricted immigration and labour's exposure to the competition of cheaply paid foreigners. At that time a conflict had broken out between organized labour and the employers. The labour forces organized the Union Labor Party, which was successful enough to win the election of November 1901, and to place its candidate in the mayor's office. Thus the Labor Party was in power at a time when Japanese immigration began vitally to affect the workingman. The opposition against the Japanese was further strengthened by the fact that the Chinese Exclusion Act was to expire in 1902. On November 22, 1901, a meeting was held at which were discussed: "Some Reasons for Chinese Exclusion," "Meat versus Rice," "American Manhood against Asiatic Coolieism, Which Shall Survive?" Not only the Chinese were attacked but also the Japanese. Although in the beginning it was emphasized that there was no prejudice against Orientals and that the motive was only an economic one, racial feelings were appealed to almost immediately. The "treacherous, sneaking, insidious, betraying and perfidious nature and characteristics of the Mongolian race" were emphasized, and the "skulking, meanly servile, and immoral" Mongolian immigrants were exposed. Japan's successes in the

Russo-Japanese War and the warning by Kaiser William II of the "Yellow Peril" increased the apprehension in California. A real invasion of Japanese immigrants was anticipated as a result of the war. Meanwhile, in 1901, 5249 Japanese had arrived; 14,455 in 1902; 20,041 in 1903; and 14,382 in 1904.

During these incipient agitations and particularly in the year 1900—when the Orientals as well as the Americans were threatened by the outbreak of bubonic plague, and the Japanese and Chinese, being Asiatic races, were dealt with in a discriminatory manner—the Japanese in San Francisco often met together to formulate plans for self-defence. The result was the organization of a community council which became the first Japanese Association of America (August 1900). This example was followed in other places.

The San Francisco *Chronicle* in February 1905 carried on a vigorous campaign against the "little yellow man," and the state legislature passed a resolution demanding of Congress that action be taken immediately to restrict the further immigration of Japanese labourers. A campaign was started in which boycotts of the Japanese and of merchants and manufacturers employing Japanese were urged. A Japanese exclusion society was organized and held an anti-Japanese convention on May 7, 1905. After the earthquake (1906)—when municipal affairs were in a chaotic situation and law and order were not maintained—assaults were made on Japanese residents. Japanese stores and restaurants were invaded, burglarized, and destroyed. Thousands of new immigrants had arrived, and, in an effort to find new homes and business locations, many Japanese who had been affected by the disaster invaded the western districts of San Francisco which hitherto had been "white man's land." Japanese restaurants were flourishing during the reconstruction of the city. With the plea, "White men and women, patronize your own race," a new boycott was proclaimed. Many Japanese left the city for southern California. Constant war talk and sensational spy stories provoked a state of high emotional tension. In the same year objection was raised to the presence of Japanese children in the schools. On October 11, 1906, the Board of Education of San Francisco required that the 93 Japanese children enrolled in various public schools attend the Oriental school, formerly used by the Chinese alone. The agitation of organized labour had grown to an anti-Japanese campaign in which the municipal government, controlled by the unions, participated. The government was trying to distract public opinion from its corrupt management by making the Japanese the scapegoat. In 1907 the secret "gentlemen's agreement" restricted immigration but, because of lack of faith in the "honour" of the Japanese Government, agitation continued. In 1905, 11,021 Japanese had entered; in 1906, 14,243. In 1907—the year of the "gentlemen's agreement" and, at the same time, of a severe economic panic—30,824 Japanese arrived; in 1908, 16,418. Cries were raised: "We are going to be overrun!" and "California shall not become the Caucasian graveyard!"

In February 1908—during a period in which relations between the United States and Japan were dangerously tense because of Manchuria—the Central Labor Council of Seattle sponsored the first international convention of the Asiatic Exclusion League of North America, which had a membership in California alone of 110,000. By May 1909 the League consisted of 238 affiliated bodies, mainly labour organizations. In March 1908 an Anti-Japanese Laundry League was organized which attempted to prevent the issuance of licences to the Japanese, to reduce their patronage by skilfully appealing to race prejudice, and to prevent Japanese from securing laundry equipment. The potential abilities of the Japanese were feared. The thought of a rapidly growing population, composed of highly efficient persons integrated into a powerful national machine, aroused apprehension. California legislative activities became more and more threatening to the Japanese. As a result of all this agitation the Japanese in 1909 combined their local Japanese Associations of America into one organization for the purpose of protecting their interests.[1] This organization comprised some forty locals in northern California and Colorado.

Several circumstances intensified the ill feeling. In the first place these Japanese associations frequently appealed to the Japanese Government for help. In the second place "impudent" Japan interfered on behalf of these Japanese, who from the American standpoint were *immigrants,* but who by their own government were regarded as *colonists,* in whose whereabouts and activities its feudal paternalism evinced an unusual interest, and for whom it displayed an extraordinary solicitude. The steps taken by Tokyo prompted the Federal Government to try to influence the situation in California, which again irritated the local public opinion to a high degree. All talk about "the rights of Japan" disgusted the Californian thoroughly! Had the Japanese leaders in California tried to come to some arrangement with the local whites—this would have been difficult, of course—it would not have stirred up so much violent emotion. Now the issue of states' rights, especially since there was a Democratic president in Washington (1913),

[1] In 1920 there were a hundred such associations in the United States and Hawaii. In 1924 there were four "main branches," to wit: (1) the Japanese Association of America, at San Francisco (with 38 affiliated local branches in central and northern California); (2) the Central Japanese Association of Southern California, at Los Angeles (with 20 affiliated local associations in southern California); (3) the Northwest American Japanese Association at Seattle (with 14 affiliated local bodies in Washington and one in Montana); (4) the Japanese Association of Oregon at Portland (with five affiliated local associations in Idaho); and three independent associations in Colorado, two in Arizona, one in Utah, one in Texas, one in Illinois, and one in New York.

created an atmosphere of hysterical suspicion of any authority or group that seemed inclined to intervene or even to influence opinion. The semi-official status given to the Japanese associations by their home government stamped them in the eyes of the public as tools of Japanese imperialism. Every Japanese was readily believed to be conniving with the Japanese Government for the ultimate destruction of America. This spectre made California pass the discriminatory land law of 1913, despite the opposition of President Wilson.

Labour organizations, military and patriotic organizations (the American Coalition of Patriotic Societies with its affiliated societies), and retail merchants' organizations combined in their attack on the Japanese. The Japanese were undesirable aliens; cultural and biological assimilation was impossible. Their patriotic self-conceit was an obstacle to amalgamation. Their low standard of living threatened the American workingman; their birth-rate was a danger to California as a white man's country. They introduced pagan cults into Christian America. Racial undesirability was emphasized, rather than racial inferiority. Ineligibility to citizenship was made the motivation for discrimination.

On the other hand the Federal Council of Churches of Christ, with its spokesman, the Reverend Sidney L. Gulick (formerly of Doshisha University, Kyoto, Japan),[2] H. A. Miller,[3] and Dr. Herbert B. Johnson, superintendent of the Pacific Japanese Mission of the Methodist Episcopal Church, were opposed to the exclusion of Japanese immigrants; the interests of Christianity in Japan were at stake. The Commission on International Peace and Good Will, the Commission on Relations with the Orient, the Pacific ports Chambers of

[2] Author of *The American-Japanese Problem* (1914), *American Democracy and Asiatic Citizenship* (1918), and *Toward Understanding Japan* (1934).

[3] Author of *The Japanese Problem in the United States* (1915).

Commerce, the importing and exporting houses, the firms having international trade relations, the California Fruit Growers, and the California Farmers Co-operative Associations also fought Japanese exclusion.

The new wave of anti-Japanese agitation since 1919—again in a period of international friction between Japan and the United States—revived the Exclusion League. Agitation led finally to the passing of the California Alien Land Law (1921) and its amendment of 1923—according to which a Japanese who did not own land previously could work it legally only as a hired labourer—and to the passing of the federal act of 1924, which excluded from immigration all aliens ineligible to citizenship. An attempt to bar the Japanese from fishing in the coastwise waters of California was frustrated by the cannery interests, which realized that such a law would injure American capital and kill the cannery business of the state, an industry dependent on Japanese fishermen.

Since that time the situation has changed little. Anti-Japanese feeling is still rather strong, although it is no longer voiced in violent forms. From time to time, stilled passions in California for and against the Oriental are again stirred to life. Japanese sympathizers and pro-Japanese organizations, especially in the East, now spread propaganda for a repeal of the Exclusion Act and for application of the quota system to Japanese immigration. They wish to take away the Japanese feeling of resentment. Particularly since May 1930 the general depression has led foreign traders to take this stand in the name of fair play and in the hope of better business relations with the Orient. But the other party is still organized in the California Joint Immigration Committee (before 1924 the Japanese Exclusion League of California), representing the American Legion, the Native Sons of the Golden West, the State Grange, and the State Federation of Labor. Irritated by the persistent pressure from the East, it maintains its stand and issues its propaganda every time "danger" arises. It shows in its secretary, V. S. McClatchy, an unusually active and effective skill in publicity. It defends the present Exclusion Act in the interests of state and nation with their Caucasian civilization, in order that California may remain what it has always been, and God Himself intended it shall always be—the white man's paradise. Grant of the quota, it is explained, would be a foot in the door, opening the way to widespread Oriental immigration. Says the Committee: "What is now demanded in this country is a policy of dignified firmness."

Meanwhile, although virulent anti-Japanese sentiment has declined decidedly and is now more or less quiescent, the accounts in newspapers averse to the Japanese keep suspicion alive. As a matter of fact this form of propaganda does not *create* anti-Japanese sentiment; it plays on attitudes that already exist, and is primarily the expression of prevailing public opinion. However, at the same time an atmosphere of fear and hostility is worked up and perpetuated by the use of flaming headlines, by the sensational stimulation of the anti-Japanese complex in the *mores*, or just by the publication of the news, exciting as it is in itself—statements by responsible Japanese officials, accounts of Japanese advances in China, and the like. Emotional opinion feeds on sensation, and—"California is the danger zone." The stronghold of anti-Japanese opposition is still San Francisco, with its boastful "native son" patriotism and its boisterous organized labour.

The agitation for crushing Japanese competition in the rural districts by means of state or federal legislation also has not yet subsided. Periodically an attempt is launched to enact a law which would prevent any Japanese or other alien ineligible to American citizenship from engaging in farming in California. However, the advantages of the already existing land laws are doubtful. The employer never can be sure of securing a supply of Japanese labour, and yet he is uncertain of getting satisfactory help elsewhere. Banks are unwilling to lend money when farming becomes so speculative. The Japanese who co-operates with land-owner or tenant is uneasy about holding his position, as he can recover no damages if the contract is broken. Meanwhile, in many sections of California, the land law is non-operative in so far as white owners find it more advantageous to rent their land to Japanese than to farm it themselves. Though it is very difficult for a Japanese to obtain title, it is by no means impossible for him to do so, provided that his go-between is honest. Many object to these subterfuges, however, and refuse to attempt to transgress the law. Although most of the big land-owners are still in favour of the Japanese, the white labourers fear most the permanent class of Japanese agriculturists (including small land-owners, renters, leasers, foremen, and labourers who live on one ranch the year round). By working long hours and adopting a low standard of living, these Japanese have gradually developed control of many of the important agricultural industries and the most fertile areas. Of chief concern to whites is the crushing competition this class of people is giving to the white rural population. Nowadays it is in the rural regions that most of the outbursts of racial feeling occur, especially in districts where the pioneer code is not forgotten and the frontier spirit is not yet lost. Here signs are sometimes placed alongside the road warning the Japanese that this is a "white man's country," that "no Japs are wanted," and that "Japs better not have the sun set on them here." On the other hand relationships between individuals of the different racial groups, even in the rural districts, are often amicable. Under these circumstances every fresh agitation is dreaded lest the aroused feelings provoke animosity and disturb the well-established goodwill.

In one respect the opposition has been very successful: there are relatively few skilled tradesmen among the Japanese. With a tradition against employing Orientals in factories and shops, and with strong opposition when fifteen Japanese cobblers were employed by the owner of a shoe factory in San Francisco (1890), employers for fifty years have generally sought to employ only white persons. The doors seldom have been re-opened to the Asiatic races.

It was stated in the first chapter that San Francisco is the city for the Chinese. Just so is Los Angeles the city for the Japanese. In 1930 the Japanese in southern California numbered 45,487, out of the total of 97,456 in California—70.2 per cent of the total Japanese population in the continental United States. The number of Japanese in Los Angeles increased from 23,000 in 1926 to 29,500 in 1927, and from 31,150 in 1930 to over 35,000 in 1935.

The same urbanizing process is going on elsewhere. In the state of Washington about 70 per cent of the Japanese are concentrated in King and Pierce Counties, which contain the two large cities of Seattle and Tacoma. The Japanese have withdrawn gradually from the wheat-growing sections, where the use of expensive and heavy machinery has been increasingly introduced. In Oregon about half have settled in Multnomah County, in which Portland is situated.

As for Japanese businesses in the city of Los Angeles, since 1924 the number which cater to white Americans as well as to other races—in contrast to those which deal more exclusively with Japanese—has steadily increased (groceries, hotels, restaurants, fruit stands, barber shops, flower shops, nurseries, cleaning and dyeing establishments, and so on). These businesses are very small as a rule, and seldom employ anyone who is not a Japanese. The wife acts as partner and the children frequently as helpers. In Los Angeles, Japanese business has surmounted the injury caused by the anti-Japanese agitation of 1920, when the stores were stoned and defaced. On many occasions police protection was necessary. Since this time aggressive race antipathy has disappeared, and the one-time anti-Japanese agitators are today the friendliest towards the Japanese. In Los Angeles the Japanese do not live in a solid segregated area; they are eager to enter the best neighbourhoods. "Japtown," and "Little Tokyo" have not the same significance as "Chinatown."

The businesses of Japanese in San Francisco, however, cater very largely to Japanese. Before the anti-Japanese agitation extensive business with whites was carried on in restaurants, laundries, and shoe-repairing shops. The first were badly injured by boycotts and have never recovered. As to the laundries and shoe-repairing shops, they have been hard hit by the competition of large laundries and by chains of shoe-cobblers. New enterprises to secure patronage from other social groups have not developed, and—as is also the case elsewhere—the second generation is deserting Japanese stores for those where goods of wider variety and more up-to-date styles are sold.

The Japanese community in Gardena district (Gardena Valley) has never had white patronage and is practically self-sufficient, independent of the white race in every way. It is amply supplied with its own stores, professional people, publications, and cultural and educational activities. There is even a tendency to exclude American activities. In Walnut Grove (Sacramento County) the business and professional Japanese in no way enter into competition with the white population, as they cater exclusively to their own people and to transient Filipino labour.

Fresno shows a rather interesting situation. This town is divided into two parts, one "west" and one "east" of the railway tracks. "West of the tracks" is the foreign-born residential section, in which at least thirty different nationalities are represented. Most of the businesses there are in the hands of Italians, Japanese, Chinese, Mexicans, and Filipinos. Three Japanese seem to be particularly successful; their places get much of the Mexican and Filipino trade. Peculiarly enough, the Armenians are not segregated, doing business and living on the east, native-born side of the tracks. The American-born whites found in the foreign (west) section of the town belong to the poorer class and are mostly of a low type. Vulgar white women display an arrogant, rude attitude when trading in the Japanese stores, but it is the Negroes who most openly exhibit a feeling of superiority to the Japanese.[4] Although racial prejudice is not absent "east of the tracks," the second-generation Japanese with their taste for things American often turn away from the Japanese stores and "go over the tracks."

Taken as a whole, the Japanese general merchandise stores, especially in the smaller communities, are often behind the times in style of goods and in prices. Business difficulties and failures are proportionately high because of poor management. Sometimes business methods are influenced by national characteristics, and competition becomes a personal matter. In case a tradesman's honour is at stake, he presses small claims instead of arranging for a suitable compromise.

Another interesting feature of the population trend is that, while in recent years the number of native-born Japanese has declined, half of the Japanese population of California in 1930 was American-born.

As among the Chinese, the relationships between the older

---

[4] This is, however, not the general attitude. In some places the relations between Negroes and Japanese are sympathetic; in other places the Negroes keep more apart from the rest of the population.

generation (*issei*) and the second-generation Japanese [5] (*nisei*) are very difficult. In the first place there is the clash between two civilizations, two philosophies. In Old Japan the social unit is the family; the individual has no position in society except as a member of a family which centres around the father. The father is always served first anywhere. If a married couple walks down the street, the wife is always seen a few feet behind the husband, modestly following. She knows that her first and foremost virtue should be obedience and that she must sacrifice her own desires to her husband and to the general welfare of the family. Marriage is a family affair—love begins with marriage. Daughters are carefully chaperoned and are permitted little freedom before marriage. Here the individualism of the younger generation revolts. Now youthful love affairs often result in hasty marriages without the previous consultation of parents. The American-born Japanese girl finds it hard to appreciate the lack of independence for which a Japanese wife is praised. The close-knit family system is breaking down in America.

The older generation, which in the early days worked under Japanese foremen, has only a very imperfect knowledge of English. Due to the difference in language, discipline has become almost impossible. The children, who have to assume the role of interpreter for their parents and do business for them, are thrown into a position of unnatural importance and feel contempt for the Old-World ways. Then, too, the children are aware that their legal status often is utilized in order to get around the Alien Land Law. The parents know only the Japan of twenty or more years ago and are not familiar with the changes that have taken place in the cities of the mother country, where a more organic adaptation has developed. The

[5] "Americans of Japanese extraction" would be a better term.

only thing they know of, or are interested in, is work. Recreation is a waste of time or downright idleness. Hence the parents come into conflict with the younger generation, which in school has learned the modern customs and ideas but has had little contact with the better American families. The younger generation often looks askance at the peculiar habits and customs of its parents, even ridiculing the traditional Japanese manners and etiquette (bow, prostration, tea ceremonial), or mocking at the round-about Japanese way of expression, which does not allow blunt negatives or direct refusals that will hurt the feelings of others. The young Japanese are prone to be ashamed of their race and their homes, to which they will not take their American friends. Their one desire is to lose their racial, national, or linguistic identities, and to become an integral part of the American people as soon as possible. They refuse to observe the customary religious practices (mourning ceremonies, putting food and flowers in front of the shrines and on the graves of their deceased relatives), jeer at Shintoism and Buddhism, and prefer to be Christians. They want to enjoy this life, want play and recreation, and do not understand why there should not be free social intercourse between the sexes. The girls especially cannot understand why they cannot go to dances as often as do American girls. But dancing is still a moral issue even in the leading westernized cities in Japan: Tokyo, Kobe, Osaka. All the dance halls in Tokyo must be closed at eleven o'clock at night. The metropolitan police prohibit the dancing of married women, the reason being that it is indecent for them to be seen embraced by men not their husbands. Therefore the professional dance halls are frequently visited and raided by police officers, detectives, and rampant "patriots" who dash in, usually with naked blades in hand.

This being the case in Japan itself, it is easy to imagine the horror felt by the older generation in America over the activities of the younger. In the older minds the younger generation is too independent, has no respect, and does not acknowledge any superior authority because of its "democratic" ideas. Being practically ignorant of the "American" ways, with which the public school has acquainted their children, the parents have lost their traditional control, and are worried by the conspicuous lack of reverence and of filial piety on the part of their offspring. A similar judgment was passed on the second-generation Japanese by the Japanese in Japan during the Japanese-American student conferences in Japan in August 1934. The Japanese were much shocked to find their American-born and American-educated brothers bluff and discourteous, disinterested in Japanese art and architecture and wishing only to know how much these beauties had cost.

The tragic phase of the situation is that to American society these Americans of Japanese extraction are still Japanese, Orientals. Like the Chinese, they are barred from the clubs, fraternities, and sororities of the American schools. They are not allowed to dance with American girls. In some places ordinances prohibit the Japanese from public golf links, tennis courts, and swimming pools, though this is by no means a general rule. There is no discrimination against the Japanese at hotels and restaurants, and in public conveyances. In San Francisco, however, they are refused admission to the public dance halls and to one public beach on east San Francisco Bay. Students often find difficulty in getting room and board in the "white" residential sections. The Y.M.C.A. in California has Chinese and Japanese branches. In the San Francisco Y.M.C.A. a few Japanese on the gymnasium floor do not seem to create difficulty, but a large number immediately changes the situation. Even one Japanese in the swimming pool brings resignations from American members. In the theatres Japanese meet unequal and unpleasant treatment, all the "Orientals" (Japanese, Chinese, Filipinos) being put, together with the Mexicans, in a special section.

The Japanese feel that they are discriminated against; high-school boys and college men feel handicapped because of their race. With the energetic young Japanese this arouses the conviction that they must excel in order to get positions. Another quite common and natural reaction is that the individual, so often cast aside just because he is a Japanese, feels like avoiding Americans as much as possible. If his personal experiences do not create a "what is the use" attitude of resignation, they may develop in him, through a process of compensation, an excessive show of pride in being a Japanese. The trouble is that American schools have educated the young Japanese to American ideals and to the American mode of thinking, to the social caste of a white-collar job. Their fathers' callings no longer satisfy them. Intermarriage with the white group is prohibited in California; as a matter of fact there are few interracial marriages even in states where they can be lawfully performed. On the other hand the marriage problem for the Japanese is not so acute as with the Chinese or Filipinos because of the better distribution of the sexes.

These Americanized Japanese, as a group, are lost for Japan. Japanese from Japan resent the ease with which the American-born have accepted their inferior status in American society. They have no honour! The Japanese employers often object to employing them because of their lack of "character" and because of their lack of knowledge of the Japanese language and moral standards.

Since the Immigration Act of 1924 a new spirit has touched the older generation; their patriotism has grown. Loyal to their empire across the sea, they send money to Japanese institutions and welfare organizations as funds and donations. This is especially true since September 1931. On the other hand the modern chauvinistic movements in Japan begin to take an interest in the American-born Japanese. Education in Japan is encouraged. Now 10,000 second-generation Japanese from America are attending schools in Japan; but out of the 1000 American-born living in Tokyo, 600 are constantly followed by police detectives, their names being recorded in the blacklist as depraved young people. Proper guidance and supervision of the students is now being organized. This is the reason why the parents no longer object to sending their children to Japan. The Kwanto Gakuin, the Aoyama Gakuin, and Waseda University, are open to American-born Japanese students. Courses are offered to them under favourable conditions. Under the auspices of the Kaigwai-Kyoiku-Kyokwai (Association for Education Abroad) a special second-generation boarding school has been established, of which the well-known statesman, Viscount Kikujiro Ishii, is the president.

In America itself, the growing national consciousness on the part of the resident Japanese manifests itself in two ways: the increased interest in religion, especially Buddhism and Shinto, and the renewed school movement.

Formerly the Americans had opposed these Japanese-language schools as teaching anti-American ideas to the children. Therefore the Japanese Educational Society of San Francisco decided in 1912 that education in the American public schools should be compulsory for those persons destined to remain in this country permanently, while the *gakuin* (the Japanese-language school) should limit its scope to the instruction of the Japanese language as a supplementary training for the *nisei* (second-generation Japanese). In 1913 the same association announced its goal to be the education of the child who was to live and die in America in the spirit of the instruction received in the public schools of America. In 1919 a general conference of the Japanese Associations of the Pacific Coast established an Educational Research Bureau to prepare special textbooks for the American citizens of Japanese ancestry. At that time it was felt necessary to supplement the knowledge of the children as regards Japan, its history, and its culture.

In 1926 there were only 2798 pupils in 40 Japanese-language schools in the nine counties of southern California; now there are 117 *gakuins* with an enrolment of over 9000. More and more, the parents have come to regard these schools as a means of cultural defence, a means of keeping the children for themselves and for their civilization. Therefore, it is not enough that the children learn only the Japanese language; they should also learn the moral code of Japanese chivalry (*bushido*) and the Japanese appreciation of loyalty, justice, and patriotism, along with the value of self-control, self-suppression, honour, and "the right." *Jyudo* and *kendo*, as taught in the schools, serve the same purpose (personality training).

The *gakuin* is the parents' answer to the closed-door policy of American society. The school's task is to prepare them for a position in Japanese business life, which is regarded as their only possible future. *Bushido* should enable them to endure the hardships of the economic and social struggle and to overcome a feeling of inferiority. It will be interesting to watch the future development of these schools. Other immigrants (Dutch, German, Scandinavian, etc.) have tried by means of the school to save the children for the parents and the native traditions, but practically all of these schools have died out during the last few generations. The younger Japanese children attend the language schools as a matter of course, just as they attend the American schools. Yet a feeling of dislike is prevalent. After a day of study in the public school, the children must proceed to the language school for several hours of further instruction, while their American schoolmates can indulge in recreational activities. Among the older children there is a very definite trend away from these schools. At any rate the experience of the last twenty years has been that these schools have been unsuccessful in their primary function—that of imparting a knowledge of the Japanese language to American-born children of Japanese descent. This fact also may explain the willingness on the part of the Japanese parents to send their children to Japan for their education.

At the bottom of all these educational efforts is the conflict between the older and younger generations. In childhood, as the Japanese children begin to make contacts with the various phases of American life through the school, they gradually drift away from their parents, trying to become as fully American as possible. They regret only that they cannot do away with their identity altogether. But as they grow older, they are sometimes rebuffed by the white group; then they tend to revert to the parental group and to develop gradually an appreciation for their parental culture, on which basis the older generation hopes to develop in them a national pride. As pupils they are liked by white teachers; but as a result of a political scare over Japan, the prejudice on the West Coast as a whole is much stronger against the Japanese than against the Chinese. This is also because the latter more often confine themselves to non-competitive jobs.

The prejudice against the Japanese has found expression in the California school laws, in which it is stated:

The governing body of the school district shall have power to establish separate schools for Indian children and for children of Chinese, Japanese, or Mongolian parentage.

When separate schools are established for Indian children or children of Chinese, Japanese, or Mongolian parentage, such Indian children or children of Chinese, Japanese, or Mongolian parentage must not be admitted into any other school.[6]

The interesting thing about these clauses is, in the first place, that the term "children of Mongolian parentage" is meant to include Filipinos, who are not explicitly mentioned because of the special relationship between the United States and the Philippine Islands. If explicit mention of them had been made, objections might have been raised by the Federal Government. As a matter of fact Filipinos are not of Mongolian parentage, but the clause is none the less effective for them. The same is true of the term "Indian children," which does not apply to American Indians but here means Mexicans. The term is only a subterfuge for avoiding conflict with the existing treaty between Mexico and the United States.

Finally, it is only fair to state that the California State Department of Education is not in favour of discrimination and tries to discourage segregation as far as possible. However, power in this respect is in the hands of the governing bodies of the local school districts. Indeed, segregation, although not general, exists, sometimes openly, sometimes in a more concealed way. The school area may be limited so as to include the quarters in which one or more "objectionable" nationalities are living; the "white" children who happen to be in the same area are allowed to go to school elsewhere. Of course the local school boards are dependent upon the public opinion of their district. Sometimes pedagogic reasons are given for segregation: the white children are supposedly being retarded because

[6] School code of the State of California, Division III. Part I, Chapter I, Article I, Clauses 3.3 and 3.4.

of the language handicap of the Japanese. So it happens that, in a number of elementary schools throughout the state, there are rooms with none but Oriental pupils, or there are separate classes in the lower grades for Orientals. Sometimes, however, prejudice is openly acknowledged as the real reason. In Florin "there were getting to be more Japs than white children in the school. The principal was letting Japs crowd our boys off the grammar-school team just because they could play better baseball. The towns around us began to razz our kids because of that, and that created antagonism toward the Japs. You know we have a low grade of Jap here. Even in their own country they are looked down on as a class. They haven't got much ability. Well, we couldn't stand for it any longer, so we separated our schools. . . ."

NOTE: In a report of the California State Commissioner of Labor dated May 29, 1910, it was stated that Japanese or some form of labour of a similar character—capable of independent subsistence and quick mobilization, submissive to instant dismissal and entailing no responsibility upon the employer for continuous employment—was absolutely necessary in the California orchard, vineyard, and field if these vast industries were to be perpetuated and developed. Such labour had to be drawn from sources beyond the United States. With the expansion of intensive agriculture the need for this type of help was still more keenly felt. The immigration of Chinese and Japanese had been stopped; aside from southern Negroes (1910–16) for the developing cotton culture and some Hindus (1908–17), Filipinos and Mexicans filled the gap.

Filipino immigration was only an incident, and it is not important for the consideration of the actual situation. A discussion of the problems connected with it would be out of place here. In the Appendix is a brief note on Filipino immigration to the Pacific Coast.

CHAPTER III

Mexicans and Indians

THE census of 1930 found nearly 1,500,000 persons born in Mexico living in the United States. Since then the widespread depression has stopped new immigration from Mexico, and approximately 300,000 have gone back to their homeland. However, the Mexicans still represent a factor of great importance in the labour supply.

Since 1908 Mexican labour has been on record as participating in the development of southern California; in 1916 Mexicans appeared as track labourers on the railroads of the Middle West; and since 1923 they have entered in large numbers the industries of Chicago and the Calumet region. In 1928 they constituted approximately 43 per cent of the track labour on the principal railroads within the latter area, and formed 11 per cent of all employees in a group including most of the important plants in the steel and meat-packing industries. There the Mexicans have replaced white labourers, and in later years, to a smaller extent, they have also replaced Negroes. In some instances the strong race antipathy towards Negroes has actually increased the employment opportunities of Mexicans. However, prejudice also attaches to them. Dark colour appears as a handicap to employment not only in food industries but in other industries where the person in control of employment has strong feelings upon the subject. In these cases the handicap bars darker Mexicans, but the lighter Mexicans are accepted. Sometimes it is the workingmen who object to working beside either Negro or Mexican labourers. Underlying this disinclination is also economic hostility. The prejudice of the other workers prevents the Mexicans from rising beyond a certain point. Mexicans sometimes try to pass for Spanish, and Negroes for Mexicans, in order to get employment.

The typical Mexican immigrant, however, is still a seasonal labourer. The ranchers need great numbers of labourers for only limited seasons. The result is that, for the rest of the time, the workers depend on relief, which represents a considerable drain on public funds and charity organizations. For the employers the Mexican is a necessary adjunct to the labour supply in the United States, an addition, satisfactory on the whole, to the low-scale wage group regarded as necessary for economic progress. Organized labour accuses the Mexican of a tendency to accept wages below the minimum standard set by trade unions.

"Cheap labour" is a term of ill repute. When unskilled immigrant labour is desired, interested persons appearing before Congressional committees are usually careful—if necessary they are cautioned—not to ask for "cheap labour," but rather to deny that the desired labour is "cheap." Nevertheless some industries need it for their very existence. Plentifulness and cheapness of field labour encourage extension of acreage, overproduction, and consequent decrease in price, which in turn prevents a rise in income. For this reason small farmers are often opposed to unlimited Mexican immigration.

Much of the Mexican labour in California migrates up and down the length of the state the year round, following the crops as it is needed: grapes in Fresno; Valencia oranges, nuts, beets, and beans in Orange County; naval oranges in Riverside County; cotton, lettuce, melons, and grapefruit in the Imperial Valley; tomatoes and asparagus wherever they may be found; pears, peaches, and apples in the Sacramento Valley; and so on, and on. In the meantime, there is some street work to be had here and there. Others keep employed more than half their time within a single county. In Orange County, for example, there are sugar beets, oranges, apricots, lemons, beans, walnuts, etc., to be harvested at different seasons. There may be but a few weeks of unemployment between seasons.

Other Mexicans extend their migrations far outside the borders of the state. In the spring of each year some thousands of Mexican families migrate as contract labourers to the sugar-beet fields. They flow into the valleys of Colorado, Nebraska, Idaho, and Wyoming; tongues of the advancing flood enter parts of Montana, South Dakota, Iowa, and Minnesota, some reaching as far east as Michigan. In late October and November the tide recedes southward. Each annual wave has left its residue of Mexicans, who winter on the farms or in the towns of the beet country, or in the northern cities, to await there the re-opening of beet work in the spring. The expansion of beet production, particularly during and after the World War—together with curtailment of the supply of Germans, Russians, Poles, Belgians, and other Europeans who previously performed most of the manual labour connected with the growing of sugar beets—has evoked this periodic migration. Many Mexicans dovetail beet work with coal mining, but the irregularity of employment is still one of the most serious problems connected with beet labour. The long winter of unemployment is particularly severe and difficult. Work in the beet fields is disagreeable. Since it is generally shunned by native Americans, labourers must be imported.

In the autumn, cotton picking attracts other waves of immigrants. Large numbers of Mexican labourers go to Arizona, and others follow the cotton harvest beginning in the lower

Rio Grande Valley of Texas or at Corpus Christi and moving north to the Panhandle and even on to Oklahoma.

Thousands of Mexicans go in the spring from the American Southwest to the farthest points where railroads may want them—in brisk times as far as Oregon, Montana, Michigan, New York, and Florida; with the decline of maintenance work in the fall, they return southward.

With the exception of those Mexicans employed in the industries, who are predominantly young unmarried men, the whole family works together. In the walnut season, for instance, entire Mexican families go out to the California groves in trucks or wagons, buggies or Fords, and camp there until the picking season is over. The women and children pick up the nuts, while the men shake the trees and load the sacks. It is a generally accepted principle that a woman must either do field work herself or produce workers to take her place.

It goes without saying that this migrating labour offers peculiar difficulties from an educational point of view. The children either do not attend school during the seasons, or they invade local schools in overwhelming numbers, to leave when the parents move on. Sometimes fathers, employers, and time merchants combine to keep children out of school and to bring pressure on the school authorities to ignore the compulsory attendance law. County superintendents, afraid of losing office in the next election, are not willing to enforce the law. The family contract system of labour is the great obstacle. The harvesting of sugar beets in Colorado, for example, is paid for by the ton. The rate paid is so low that the father must call upon his whole family to help him. In most of rural southern Texas there is neither pretence nor effort to enforce on Mexican children the state compulsory attendance law. For those Mexican children who do attend school, the facilities in most respects are obviously below those provided for American children. This is true with respect to buildings, equipment, and room space per pupil; frequently with respect to the salary scale of teachers; and frequently, though by no means always, with respect to the qualifications of teachers. Those who have completed the grades offered in the "Mexican" school are not permitted to transfer to the "American" school; either another grade (without adequate equipment) is added to the instructional duties of the teachers in the Mexican school, or the pupils just end their schooling, or go elsewhere for it. State aid is apportioned to school districts on the basis of the number of children shown by the school census. The result is that the Mexicans are diligently enrolled on the census, while the revenues are applied principally to the education of the American children. The practice is justified mainly by the fact that the Americans are the principal taxpayers. The prevailing opinion is that: "Educating the Mexican is educating him away from his job. . . . He learns English and wants to be a boss. He doesn't want to grub. . . . Somebody has to transplant onions. It is a bad task. What would we do if 50 per cent of the Mexican pupils showed up? It would take more teachers and school houses. We would not have enough lumber for school houses nor enough teachers in Texas, and who wants that? . . ." The dominant view of the local Americans is that it is undesirable to educate the Mexicans. Economic, moral, religious, and biological arguments are adduced in support of this opinion.

Not only in Texas, and to a somewhat smaller extent in California's Imperial Valley, but also in north-eastern Colorado there is the tendency to segregate the Mexican children in school. The same segregation is found in other respects. Social relations between Americans and Mexicans are extremely few. Often American girls in Colorado express a prejudice against social intercourse with Mexicans and are particularly emphatic in their opposition to intermarriage which, as a matter of fact, is extremely rare. In California, however, intermarriages between Mexican immigrants and the members of other races sometimes take place. Ignorant Mexicans marry low-grade Negroes, Japanese, Filipinos, Europeans, or Americans. Interracial marriages on a higher level also occur.

On the side of the Mexicans there is also prejudice against things American. The freedom and independence in this country bring the children into conflict with their parents. In Mexico no girl or young woman would go out alone in the evening. American girls go unchaperoned to parties with young men; Mexican girls in the United States respond at once to such freedom. In becoming "American" they may become "delinquent."

In the towns separation of domicile is general: the typical Mexican area is "the other side of the tracks." In the Southwest the "Mexican" community is sometimes the original settlement; the "Americans" have come later. In this case the "Anglos" sometimes strive to remove the Mexicans, as the Mexican area is judged to be an "eyesore." Some want "to drive the Mexicans out." Among ranchers there is a tendency to locate the beet labourer's house at a distance from the rancher's own house in order to diminish the personal contact between the two families. It is significant that Mexican farm labourers rarely eat at table with the farmer's family, although it is customary for American farmhands to do so. A few years ago barber shops, eating places, billiard parlours, and even shoe-shining stands had signs to the effect that "No Mexicans are allowed," "No Mexican patronage," "White trade only."

Although the display of such discriminatory signs has now almost wholly disappeared, in many towns it is still impossible for a Mexican to get a shave or a bite to eat.

As far as labour relations are concerned, there are often conflicts between employer and employee, arising from a different philosophy of life. The active, energetic, materialistic American wants plentiful labour in a hurry when he wants it, and at the lowest price. The Mexican enjoys savouring life; he wants to labour only when he desires, and in amounts and intensity to suit him. The Mexican peon is plantation-minded. In his homeland he has lived in the hacienda village and has been fashioned into a more or less docile and dependent creature. He has not been trained to assume responsibility. He has not had much of this world's goods for which to become responsible. He has not been taught to save; he has had little or nothing to save. Stimulated to come to the United States chiefly by the reports of high wages, he works with the idea of frequently taking a few days off in order to enjoy the fruits of his labour. He lives so largely in the present that time has no particular meaning to him. With him time is not commercialized as with us. On the other hand he is willing to do much of the work scorned by the American labourer. Moreover, the Mexican with his very low standards of living is not "always wanting something" as is the white or even the Negro; therefore, many landlords like him better as a tenant. He knows "his place." This attitude plays a part in the process of displacement in the farm tenancy of Texas.

Apart from these Mexican immigrants, there are two other groups of people styled "Mexican" that require separate mention. First, there are, especially in southern California, the educated and sophisticated political refugees from Mexico who belong to the better classes (*criollos* and *mestizos*). Second, in southern Colorado and New Mexico particularly, and to a lesser extent in Texas, Arizona, and California, there are large numbers of persons culturally Spanish, whose mother tongue is Spanish, whose ancestry is Spanish or Mexican, and whose forefathers for generations inhabited the area before the Americans invaded their territory and "manifest destiny" included it in the United States.

The average American does not discriminate between these three groups and labels them all as "dirty greasers," "unshaven, unbathed, illiterate aliens." Sometimes the Americans of Spanish descent as a class are given credit for being better educated, for using better Spanish and better English, for being better dressed and of a higher type than the Mexicans from Old Mexico, but as individuals very few Americans distinguish them. On the other hand these Spanish-Americans are very proud, both of their ancestry, which they trace back, at least collectively, to the days of Spanish colonization of New Mexico, and of their United States citizenship. They claim superiority to the Mexicans on grounds of superior language, education, cleanliness, and culture. They feel themselves to be Americans and at least a hundred years ahead of the Old Mexico Mexicans. They claim that the Mexicans have brought them into disrepute with the Americans.

Of course, the nearly 1,500,000 people born in Mexico that the census of 1930 found in the United States, and more particularly the thousands of migrating families among them, form, as a whole, a socially disorganized crowd. Constantly migrating, they often live under almost incredible conditions. They live in houses abandoned as unfit for human habitation, in outhouses that have no facilities for housekeeping, in living quarters congested to the saturation point, and without toilet conveniences. They live in huts, in sheds, in barns, in tents, in smokehouses, under trees, under strips of canvas, and in cars. Such circumstances do not encourage orderly behaviour.

Both their personal and social life are extremely disorganized.

Still, even in these people some traits are preserved of the culture of which they were a part in their homeland, especially their love for music, dancing, and colour. The average American classifies them all as "Mexicans": the migrating transients, the second American-born generation, the proud aristocratic refugees, and the Spanish-speaking original inhabitants of the Southwest. All share in a prejudice which is composed of many elements: the aversion to "colour," social pressure against intermixture with an "inferior" race, the disdain of the conqueror for the conquered, the hatred of the frontiersman for those who are in his way, the revulsion of the matter-of-fact, unimaginative, puritanical Yankee from Roman Catholicism and Latin folkways, the contempt of the higher economic class for the lower, and the resentment born of and fostered by conflicts with raiding border bandits.

A new culture seems to be developing in southern California and New Mexico. In the city of Los Angeles is a Mexican street, "la Calle Olvera," now known as "El Paseo de los Ángeles." This remnant of early California has been reconstructed with its historic old Ávila adobe houses where Colonel John C. Frémont made his headquarters. It has cafés and colourful little booths where Mexican sweets, pottery, and other wares are sold. It is referred to as a "bit of Old Mexico" but is criticized by Mexicans because it is not a replica of any street in Mexico. Neither is it exactly as it was when Colonel Frémont arrived. Nevertheless this historic spot, which had deteriorated, has now been beautified and has become a great attraction to tourists. American cafés and restaurants feature Spanish and Mexican fiestas; many Americans have become addicted to Mexican cooking and frequent Mexican restaurants. Building in Mission style is in vogue.

This aspect of the Southwest is misleading. Granted that a

few places have genuine historic and cultural interest and that
Mission architecture is particularly suited to the climate, it
is quite apparent that commerce has decided that a Spanish
atmosphere has an actual value in dollars. It is a play attitude;
it is the Hollywood spirit; it is a real-estate venture; it is tourist
trade propaganda; but it is not the expression of a new culture.
Centring at Pomona College, there is a growing interest
among intellectuals in Mexico, in civilization, and especially
its modern developments. On the other hand much of the
goodwill thus created is annihilated by anti-religious, anti-
capitalistic, and anti-foreign tendencies in the present regime of
Mexico, which are being broadcast by the press. At any rate
interest in Mexico does not imply the desire for preserving
and reviving Mexican civilization on American soil, particularly not in such a state as New Mexico, where 50 per cent of
the population is Spanish-speaking. Here race feeling is an easy
weapon of politics, the vanities of the Spanish group and the
prejudices of the Anglo-Americans being played upon bla-
tantly by rival politicians. Even Spanish-speaking Americans
wish to forget their cultural heritage and become as thoroughly
American as possible. Such is the strain they feel imposed by
the milieu in which they are living.

The reason for this is to be sought in American self-
complacency. Not only do the rich natural resources provide
almost everything material that is needed, but also there is
a general feeling that this great country possesses everything
culturally worth while and has nothing to learn. American society does not feel any need of "foreign" co-operation; in general it feels perfectly satisfied with itself, perfectly able to
manage its own future in accordance with its own desires and
to create all the values it wants. There is an inability and an
unwillingness to look on anything foreign as worth being assimilated.

Although in our fourth chapter we shall try to analyse the psychic and social basis of this attitude, we may remark here that it is partly formed through contacts with immigrants. The average immigrant was a poor man who had to learn a great deal in order to fit into American life; he lived meanly in the poorest quarters. This inevitably created a feeling of superiority on the part of the older residents. So there is an implicit and explicit assumption that Americanization necessarily means progress. Apparently the immigrant had nothing to contribute but his labour. It was inconceivable that there could be something worth while in his cultural heritage. This superiority feeling has also inspired a missionary spirit. So it is not surprising that Americanization activities, as they are now performed by adult class work, are so often characterized by a Pharisaical, holier-than-thou approach, especially when teachers explain why immigration restriction is needed. Leaders in very respectable, very well-intentioned Americanization agencies may still be heard referring to the immigrants as "these people." There is a prevailing attitude of standing above the level of the foreigner and reaching down a kindly hand to pull him up to a higher station. Americanization work becomes in this way a sort of glorified slumming—a "Lady Bountiful" relationship. It is to the alien's own self-interest that he should "adopt our ways" for the simple reason that America is the best and the finest country in the world.

Underneath this condescending attitude is also the desire to preserve "the America our fathers knew" and the fear of losing the qualities which made America a great nation. Perhaps part of it is to be attributed to a trait in the American character which might be explained as a survival of frontier sentiments. The spirit of unyielding reliance upon self as the only stable element in a constantly shifting environment grew out of the continuous opening up of new territory and the

repeated seeking out of new homes by the people. This dominant individualism, distinguished by coarseness and strength
combined with acuteness, gives a masterful grasp of material
things and is powerful to effect great ends, but is inconsiderate
of others and of the nuances of culture.

Under these circumstances it is not surprising that there is
no appreciation for the specific cultural values of the Spanish-
speaking Southwest. It is a conquered country; the magnani-
mous conqueror is willing to hand his values over to the conquered. This also explains the attitude towards the Spanish
language. From a commercial point of view the study of Spanish is useful; as a vehicle of a foreign culture within the borders
of the United States it must disappear.

It is no wonder that this attitude prevails. America is made
up of a diversified population which pledges "allegiance to
the flag of the United States of America and to the Republic
for which it stands, one Nation, indivisible, with Liberty and
Justice for all."

The American repeating "The American's Creed" states:
"I believe in the United States of America as a Government
of the people, by the people, for the people; whose just powers
are derived from the consent of the governed; a democracy
in a republic; a sovereign Nation of many sovereign States;
a perfect union, one and inseparable; established upon those
principles of freedom, equality, justice and humanity for which
American patriots sacrificed their lives and fortunes. . . ."

In the United States there is a fairly general belief that
the language is fundamental and that the solidarity of the
people depends upon the use of the English language. "If the
[World] war drove any one lesson home, it was this need of
a common language as the basis for a loyal, unified citizenry."

This attitude explains the popular crusade after the war,
known as the Americanization movement, which saw Ameri-

canization essentially as an educational task. As soon as the first enthusiasm had burned itself out, the movement boiled down to the more simple and standardized form of language classes. It was in keeping with the general belief in education as the key to individual progress and the solution of all social ills that the difference between a member of the American nationality and the immigrant was regarded essentially as a matter of knowledge; therefore, it could be adjusted by education. So it was only natural that the main attack was on the language front. The difference in language is the most conspicuous difference between the American and the immigrant, and it is customary to consider foreigners who have not acquired the English language as unintelligent.

Evidence of the desire for unity is also the free public school, viewed in the light of the aversion to the private denominational (especially Roman Catholic) school, which is criticized as perpetuating group differences and causing a cleavage within the nation. In the same way, but to a still higher degree, the foreign-language school is regarded as an impediment to effective unity. The public school is an agency for social control, an instrument for making citizens possess like-mindedness and solidarity.

All of this is part of the desire for maintaining the American spiritual and social heritage, and explains the attitude towards the foreign language, the foreign culture, and the teaching of English. In many of the official manuals for teaching English to the foreign-born this is emphasized:

Unless there is no other way to convey the meaning to the child in English, do not resort to the use of his language.

Every time the teacher resorts to translation in making clear a word or sentence, she is making it easier for herself at the expense of the pupil's progress. The more English the pupil hears and uses, the sooner will he be able to speak.

We do not want teachers who speak Spanish to use their knowledge in dealing with Mexican children. We insist on the children speaking English in the class room, and as far as possible on the school grounds.

It is well for the teacher to have a knowledge of Spanish in order to understand the pupils and their problems in studying English and also to know if the thought is understood. However, as little as possible of the Spanish should be spoken in the English class. . . . The problem is to get the child to think in English and to express himself in English.

This opinion prevailing, it is not surprising that no special effort appears to be made to secure teachers able to speak Spanish or especially trained to teach Mexican immigrant children. So far as Spanish is taught, it is taught as a foreign language for utilitarian purposes, not for its cultural value.

Very few people appear to have any idea of the extent of the problem of teaching foreign children to read English. Outside of the teaching profession, it is regarded merely as a process of telling them how to pronounce the words and to know in a general way what they mean. Although the teachers themselves know that it is a much bigger undertaking than this, even they frequently fail to comprehend fully the difficulty of the problem, especially if they have been under the influence of the mania for intelligence tests. These seemed to confirm the already fixated opinion about the low intelligence-quotient of foreign-language children. Nowadays, however, it is realized more and more that the so-called intelligence tests really are language tests and properly can be used only as devices for comparing the achievements of pupils of the same environment. It seems almost impossible to create tests in which the language element does not affect the results. To translate English tests into Spanish, submit these to the Spanish-speaking pupils, and compare their achievements with those of the English-speaking children in the English tests—

as sometimes is done—is also useless. In the first place it is not always possible to retain the same test-element in the translation; in the second place the Spanish-speaking children have never learned Spanish as the English-speaking children have learned English. However, it is doubtless true that the test mania has strengthened the existing prejudice in a high degree and has discouraged many teachers from wasting too much energy on the instruction of the foreign-speaking child.

It would be easier to realize the difficulty of teaching English to the foreign child if it were thought of as teaching a foreign language. It is known that, although thousands of more or less mature English-speaking students spend a great many hours studying foreign languages, the number of these students who progress far enough to enjoy the literature or to express themselves fluently in these languages is not so great. This shows that the task of learning to read and to use a foreign language is hard even for mature students. How many difficulties, then, must the learning of English present to the foreign-speaking child who does not find any assistance in his life at home? Nevertheless, a large number of first-grade teachers think only of teaching the child to recognize the words in print and in script and to pronounce them correctly. They make insufficient provision for developing the meanings because they think that the children will know what the word means when they hear it pronounced. Children thus taught often become fluent oral readers. As they go on, they tend to memorize page after page, often fooling even their own teachers into believing that they understand the content.

Some thoughtful teachers have realized the difficulty and have tried to develop methods by which better results might be obtained, but such experiments are by no means general. Even professional educators do not always understand that

there is a problem. Unconsciously, it is accepted that the business of learning English is the duty of the pupil rather than
any responsibility of the teacher. Why should the tested
routine method which yields excellent results with American
children not be good enough for these people? If the result is
that the majority of these children cannot advance above the
lower grades, often even not beyond the first grade, such a
phenomenon attracts little public attention. If anyone has to
account for it, he will attribute it either to the well-known
laziness and stupidity of these children, or to a system based
on promotion according to achievement instead of promotion
according to age. He will advocate an adaptation of the school
to the needs of the social environment, which amounts to training the girls to become cooks and the boys to become gardeners.
The teacher is never to blame; she applied the time-honoured
methods.

In California, Arizona, Texas, and New Mexico individual
students and groups have become interested in this subject.[1]
The experiments which are in progress are devoted to finding
new teaching *techniques*. What is aimed at is a more effective
method of teaching English. Although a few would like to
go further and are considering the possibility of a harmonious
blending of the two civilizations, the present experiments are
of a restricted nature. Even where Spanish is used, it serves
only purely utilitarian purposes, such as a means for the teacher
to make herself better understood by the pupils. Sometimes
Mexican plays and games are used to awaken the interest of
the pupils, but as a rule the originators of these experiments

[1] Herschel T. Manuel, Carrie E. Wright, J. L. Meriam, Dr. Veverka,
Alice Cook Fuller, Basil Armour, Mrs. Muriel Goodwin Brown, George
I. Sanchez, L. S. Tireman, Sarah T. Barrows, Elma A. Neal, Ollie Perry
Storm, Genevieve Martindale, Alberta Wallace, Nona Rodee, R. T. Neidef-
fer, and others.

themselves are not convinced that, aside from some folk-lore, folk-dances, and folkways, there is a cultural background worth preserving and developing. In recent years the problem of teaching English to Spanish-speaking children has also gained the attention of the Federal Bureau of Education and the state departments of education in the Southwest.

The main purpose of all these experiments is to develop a vocabulary (by means of activities and formal instruction) on which to build the education, and to make pupils think in English. The principal difficulty will be to avoid producing a cleavage in the children's minds between home and emotional life on the one hand and school and intellectual life on the other. Other countries confronted with the same bilingual and bicultural problem have abandoned the exclusive use of the direct method. They have adopted the practice of developing the elementals with the vernacular as the medium of instruction; the "foreign" language is introduced gradually in order to effect a more perfect synthesis. This method is, however, not possible in most of the states, as the state laws prohibit the use of Spanish in the grammar school. Social and political conditions are of such nature that a change in this attitude is not likely, at least in the near future.

The most important point in these experiments is that the problem has finally been recognized and is being studied, and that this study forms an integral part of the preparation of teachers. The work done by L. S. Tireman in Albuquerque, New Mexico, deserves special mention since it also reaches the teachers actually in service.

The American attitude towards the Mexican and the indigenous Spanish culture of the Southwest is in strange contrast to the official attitude towards the Indian civilizations in New Mexico and Arizona.

It is not necessary to recall here the whole history of the

relations between the Indians and the American settlers.[2] The
Indians passed from being independent aboriginal tribes, sovereign "foreign" nations, to becoming protectorates. Tribal
sovereignty was gradually limited until the Indians became
"dependent nations" "under the immediate care and patronage" of the United States, and finally communities of "wards"
or reservation Indians. Intertribal warfare, often stimulated by
the whites; rivalry and wars between the European colonies,
in which the red men participated as allies; "Indian wars";
and diseases and epidemics, sometimes said to be propa-
gated by the whites, decimated their numbers. While the traders attracted the wrath of the Indians by cheating, sexual
irregularities, and slave raiding, the land hunger of the
frontiersmen frustrated all government policies and treaties
devised to set aside a separate Indian country. If the settlers
did not actually say that the Indians were the Hittites who
were to be driven out before the saints of the Lord, they did
accept the doctrine that "manifest destiny" must drive the Indians from the earth. Ahab never spoke kindly of Naboth. A
policy of extermination was put into practice;[3] it found its
ideology in the doctrine that "the red man withers at the touch
of civilization." The old Indian custom of exchanging presents
as a ratification of treaties developed into a form of bribery
to persuade the Indians to sign treaties and to keep peace.
Payments were also made to save them from starvation since
"it was cheaper to feed the whole flock for one year than to
fight them for one week." These treaty payments actually be-

[2] In this report I have touched on the Indian only slightly and inciden-
tally. I am fully aware that in a complete study of American race relations
much more space should be given to this particular race problem with
which even the first settlers were confronted. However, I restricted myself
to actual conditions for the understanding of which the general and historical problems are of only secondary importance.

[3] See Chapter I.

came annuities, although Congress sometimes failed to make the necessary appropriations. These annuities, the possibility of leasing their land to white settlers, the frequent forcible removals of the Indian tribes from their hunting grounds, the extinction of game, the loss of self-confidence and self-subsistence, pauperized the Indians and made them dependent on outside help. The economic basis of their existence being repeatedly destroyed, the Indian communities, surrounded on all sides by white populations, degenerated. Effective steps were not taken to educate them to citizenship or to assimilate them. Since 1887 Indians have been allowed to become citizens upon their acceptance of their allotment of tribal lands or upon their adoption of the habits of civilized life. In 1901 the members of the "Five Civilized Tribes" of Oklahoma were granted citizenship. Since 1924 all non-citizen Indians born within the territorial limits of the United States are citizens. They are located on about two hundred reservations scattered from Maine to California in twenty-two states; they comprise sixty tribes of a great variety of languages and of a variety of religions, tribal laws, and culture. Sooner or later the Indians of Wisconsin (10,000), Michigan (1200 on reservations with 6400 scattered), Minnesota (13,000), New York (6000), Wyoming (1800), Utah (1500), California (13,000), Oregon (6700), Washington (10,000), Nebraska (2000), Kansas (1500), and Oklahoma (119,000) will disappear in the "melting pot." Those of Nevada (11,000), South Dakota (23,000), Montana (12,000), and Idaho (3900) will probably be more resistant, at least for some decades. As for the Indians of Arizona (43,000) and New Mexico (21,000), the Navajos and the Pueblos, because of their isolation, still have preserved many of their peculiar cultural traits.

It is on these tribes that the Bureau of Indian Affairs has

concentrated its especial attention. The Indian boarding
schools, to which mere infants were sometimes taken by threats
and armed force, are gradually being replaced by day schools
situated in the home environment. The boarding schools
taught the pupils to despise their ancestral customs, gave them
some academic and vocational training and some hygienic
notions. As the boarding-school child was too poorly equipped
to try his luck in the white man's centres, he had no choice but
to return to Indian country and, perhaps after some vain struggle to put into use his Europeanized training, to yield to the
force of tribal opinion and "go back to the blanket." For that
life his education was of no avail. The economic conditions of
the reservations remaining the same, he was forced to adjust
himself. The day school will be a great improvement in so
far as it will preserve the connexion of the child with his
family, but the family will have to accommodate itself, as the
children will no longer be fed and clothed by the government.
At least such is the intention. However, it is a pity that this
great change is not to be introduced experimentally so that
the results can be studied at leisure.

All kinds of innovations are being thrust upon the Navajo
people. The existing decentralized authority has recently been
replaced by a centralized administration for the Navajos, for
which a capital is being built at Nee Alneeng, twenty-five miles
from Gallup, New Mexico. Moreover, as a result of the
Wheeler-Howard Act, self-government is being introduced
into the Navajo country. An organization unit of field agents
and special men has been created which will co-operate with
tribal councils, business committees, and special tribal commissions in framing a constitution. At the same time white officers are being retired and replaced by Indians, both as officials
in the Indian service and as routine workers outside the permanent staff. Indians are even being appointed as teachers in the

new experimental day schools, for which task they have never had the necessary training. They are expected to teach the Navajo language, which they have never learned to read or write and for which textbooks do not exist. Meanwhile, since the reservation is regarded as over-grazed, the number of the sheep must be reduced to less than 50 per cent of its 1933 size (1,300,000 head). Soil preservation and irrigation projects are being executed. The nomadic Navajos will be concentrated in villages; communities will be organized by Indian social workers connected with the schools. Sheep raising as a main pursuit must be abandoned. The people will have to turn to agriculture, but since only a small part of the reservation is fit for cultivation, a portion of the population will be removed.

All this is a part of "the new policy of setting the Indian to save himself," of "liberating and rejuvenating a subjugated and exploited race living in the midst of an aggressive civilization far ahead, materially speaking, of its own."

America likes to establish big works in a minimum of time. The Commissionership of Indian Affairs is a political office, the incumbent of which is subject to periodic change together with the national administration. The New Deal appropriated money for this venture which will perhaps never again be available. Soil erosion studies speak alarmingly of an economic crisis with which the Navajo nation is confronted. These several circumstances explain in part why all these drastic innovations were begun at the same time. The Indians have been neglected and often cheated; there is *periculum in mora*. The present Indian Commissioner (1935), a true friend of the Indians, feels his responsibility; he wants to do his utmost to save the Indians and their civilization.

All these projects taken as a whole mean an economic and perhaps a social revolution. Removal of some of the mountain Navajos to the malaria-infested coast plain recalls some ill-fated experiments in the history of American-Indian relationships. For the remaining Navajos the change from sheep' raising to agriculture, from nomadic to settled life, is also radical, although some generations ago the Navajos seem to have been agriculturists. Community life and self-government are also novelties. It is an open question whether the traditional chiefs will be able to meet these problems.

These innovations must be introduced and executed by the personnel that exists. Some of them are routine workers who have seen many commissioners come and go. Some are young and inexperienced Indians who have no authority whatever among their fellow-Navajos. They must make themselves and their projects acceptable to the chiefs and the elders (whom it will be hard to convince of the necessity of all these changes), and they are tied by strong sentimental and traditional ties to the direct and concrete interests of their families. Some are young white officers who have no knowledge of Navajo manners, customs, and ways of thinking.

One of the greatest difficulties is that the government's traditional Indian policy as formerly administered has not fitted the Indian for regular social intercourse with the white man and has made him entirely dependent on government aid. He cannot make his way in the general American society. He often lacks the energy for this because he knows that he can always fall back on the reservation. Sad to confess, the new policy has strengthened this tendency rather than diminished it. When relief work was started on the reservations—for which relatively high wages were paid—Indians who had actually found employment in the white man's world hurried back to the reservations. As a matter of fact, the Federal Government pours millions of dollars into these projects, paying the Indians twice as much as is customary in rural New Mexico. Never has there been so much cash in Indian hands. The result is that they have better food, better clothes, better implements and tools; some even have dilapidated automobiles. However, venereal diseases, liquor drinking, and indebtedness have also increased.

It is claimed that the new policy has already started a renaissance in Indian arts. The young Indians are painting murals on the walls of school houses and government buildings. Various government projects in 1934 provided jobs for 20,000 young Indians in addition to a quota of 14,000 Indians in the Civilian Conservation Corps (out of a total of 250,000 Indians according to the 1930 census, or 350,000 according to the current estimate of the Indian Office).

This is an artificial situation which does not provide a sound basis for the development of specific cultural values. In the past, Navajo culture has been able to resist amalgamation because of its isolation and remoteness. How long will this isolation stand in the age of the motor car and of discovery of new natural resources?

In New Mexico there is a place for a long-range programme for cultural development which includes the Spanish-speaking population *and* the Indians, who have been under strong Spanish and Mexican influence in the course of the centuries. Local Mexican arts and Indian arts are so closely related that the state supervisor of vocational instruction has made Indian studies and is co-operating with some of the teachers in the Indian schools.

However, the development of such a new bilingual civilization seems to me impossible because of the presence of the economically dominant "Anglo" group, which presses towards uniformity. To preserve in the midst of this aggressive society a distinctive Indian civilization is equally impossible. The Indians must become assimilated and find their places in American society.

In some states there is still a prejudice against the Indians; they are often associated with Mexicans; sometimes frontier sentiments survive. Some states still have legal obstacles against intermarriage, but elsewhere intermarriage is accepted. Often such marriages are regarded as "romantic" because the Indian marrying into a white family always descends from an Indian "prince." Intermarriage has been America's greatest contribution to the solution of the Indian problem. The Indian Office claims that there are still 125,000 full-blooded Indians. Other authorities regard this figure as an overestimation of 100 per cent.

CHAPTER IV

America and the Alien

THE primary attitude displayed by an ordered society towards the alien is one of distinct animosity, of contempt. Ancient Greece and ancient China regarded foreigners as uncivilized barbarians. The ancient Arabs even doubted whether the vocal sounds of the Persians could be termed a language. In Latin and other languages the concepts of "foreign" and "foe" are expressed by the same word. The in-group are "the men."

The basic motive underlying this anti-foreign attitude is that the alien is conspicuous because he is different. Even in his own group an individual who deviates from the established *mores*, who dresses or behaves differently, is likely to provoke hostility. This explains the often vehement opposition to change of any kind. Human nature is conservative, prefers the beaten path. What everybody does or says is the standard for what is right and true. If a new fashion is introduced, it is criticized; a few weeks later, when everybody wears it, it is accepted *because* everybody wears it, and therefore everybody *has* to wear it. When old pictures are looked at after some years, people wonder how such bad taste once could prevail.

Consequently, it is only natural that the alien, since he does not conform to the pattern, creates a feeling of revulsion and therefore is objectionable. He is too noisy or too dignified, too free or too reserved, too sophisticated or "just like a child," too talkative or too reticent, too gullible or too suspicious; he is too stubborn, or he "has no character." If his moral standards differ from ours, he is immoral. If he has different business methods, he is dishonest or tricky; he is distrusted because of the "unethical" way in which he conducts his trade. Any practice, any attitude, which is not customary, which is not in our code or in our social ritual, is shocking. People easily misunderstand and misinterpret foreign customs which subtly offend those habits of group taste which are somehow felt to have their roots in essential morality. Differences in behaviour are resented as evidence of mental and moral deficiency. Any deviation from the given scheme of life excites moral disapproval.

The greater the difference in cultural or social heritage, the greater is the repugnance. The experience of a difference may vary according to the way in which one makes one's contacts with the alien: as fellow-worker, employee, employer, customer, business man, neighbour, competitor, teacher of the foreigner's children, social worker, or as guest at some social function.

Within the same nation there is prejudice between people living in different parts of the country, where only slight differences in the mode of living are noticeable. In the same geographical unit prejudices exist between fellow-countrymen belonging to different strata of the society. In the old-fashioned cities of western Europe newcomers often have no access to the exclusive circles of the old families.

It is typical of these prejudices that they come to be fixated in the way the group or the individuals came to be conceived. Fixation of prejudice was often set even before contact occurred. Not what somebody does or does not do, but what he is expected to do, determines the attitude. If people know where you come from, the established opinion of what, in that case, your characteristics should be will soon discover in you the anticipated peculiarities. The prejudice, therefore, is not merely a spontaneous, unreflecting *feeling* of aversion, aroused by the perception of dissimilarity. It is also a *pre-judgment*, not based on the individual's distinctive characteristics, but rather supported, confirmed, and justified by the apperception of his differences from the in-group, by personal experiences, or by what is heard from friends, or read in the newspapers. The "foreigner" is not judged as an individual but as a member of his group.

A second element in this prejudice is that the peculiarities which are regarded as typical for certain groups are the standards for classifying others. In America eating with the knife and fork held constantly in the hands is "what lumber folks do." In western Europe eating with the fork in the right hand and the left elbow on the table or on the knee is "what people in the kitchen do." Bringing the knife to the mouth is regarded in England as a "bad German habit."

A third element in this prejudice is that if, in a desire for recognition, a person belonging to a certain group adopts habits which are regarded as distinctive of another group, such "impudent" behaviour is resented as an encroachment on the privilege of the latter group. The offender has "forgotten his place" in the social structure and is likely to provoke hostility, or he is labelled affected or a "climber." Such encroachments, of course, are often evidence of a social change which the disintegrating feudal society of the seventeenth and eighteenth centuries in Europe tried to check by discriminatory legislation with penal sanctions, thereby indicating the decay of spontaneous organic social control. In the same way the American community resents the "self-conceit" of Japanese, Armenians, Negroes, and others who do not "keep their place."

The alien, therefore, is not only conspicuous as an individual because of his appearance and his behaviour, but also is objectionable as a member of his group about whose undesirable peculiarities opinion is already fixated. He arouses still further resentment if he deviates from the customs and manners arbitrarily assigned to his group.

However much a paradox it may seem, the foreigner outside of his traditional environment is not a typical member of his group. As soon as he leaves his milieu, he also leaves behind the social control which determines his behaviour and stamps him as a member of his group.

The Englishman who strongly objects to "continental habits" rejoices in the sidewalk cafés of Paris. While, at home, he would never fail to go to church on Sunday or offend public opinion by playing tennis or cards, abroad the restraining influences weaken. The country preacher may participate in some of the allurements of the big city against which he warns his flock in his rural parish. Why when abroad do we resent being identified with a crowd of tourists, fellow-countrymen? Why does an American not always feel gratified to be considered a replica of America's Hollywood population?

The traveller is not a normal specimen of his group, for he is without the typical social control, i.e., the inner compulsion to conform to the prevailing standards of his community. The same holds true even to a greater extent for the immigrant, although he may live together with his compatriots in the same neighbourhood, and may try to maintain the old customs.

The immigrant is a product of lack of adjustment in his homeland, either because he has "lost face" there in some way and intends to begin a new life, forgetting the past, or because his opportunities at home do not accord with his spiritual, more often his economic or social, ambitions. His breaking away from the traditional social control is not merely incidental or accidental, but intentional and symptomatic. It is his rebellion against the social order at home that he expresses when he goes to the land of freedom and equality, of opportunity to rise.

But America is not a land of unrestricted freedom: it has developed its own social pattern, largely modelled after New England traditions. If, therefore, as in older days, the immigrant came from western Europe, assimilation was not too difficult. Moreover, there were in the different parts of the United States communities, settlements, where he could find people of his own descent, often even from his own home town, where he could gradually be influenced, modified, and adjusted to American conditions, and so finally identified with American society. Besides, there was formerly the frontier to take care of the unadjustable elements. In those days America was the "melting pot," although the process of integral Americanization, so far as the first generation was concerned, was slower than is sometimes realized. Even in this period apprehension manifested itself when the "bands of homeless, houseless mendicants" from Ireland invaded the country, "the deluge of paupers from Germany" flooded the American soil, and "the sweepings of English poorhouses and prisons" were "dumped" on these shores. The Puritanical tradition found particular difficulty in digesting the large quantum of Roman Catholicism among the newcomers. The nativist movement of Know-Nothingism in 1852 and later was a reaction, born of the instinct of self-preservation, against these "foreign and to a great extent anti-American" elements. Its entire creed was comprised in these two words—Americanism and Protestantism. However, the "earlier immigration" settled largely in the small towns and in the open country, where the rough and simple life was organized on an intimate and personal basis and acquaintanceship was spontaneous and inclusive. On the other hand, the "new immigration" massed in the large commercial and industrial centres because of the unavailability of free land and the better economic opportunities in cities.

Indeed, America's phenomenal development and its un-limited resources not only required and attracted, but also de-manded cheap labour. This meant more and more immigrants. Thousands upon thousands flowed into the Land of the Free, immigrants not only of the more easily adjustable type, but people from southern and eastern Europe, people of an en-tirely different tongue, of a completely different background and social heritage. During the first decade of the twentieth century they came at the rate of 900,000 persons a year.

The contrasts were too striking, the numbers too large to be digested in a short time. Such an immigration could not fail to affect the whole system of life. These heterogeneous masses could not be incorporated at once into the social body, could not immediately become an integral part of the existing or-ganization, and could not instantly participate in its character-istic values. Conflicts were bound to arise where groups with different concepts of life and different habits, traditions, and manners were forced into contact.

The nationality of the immigrants tended to determine their calling or at least their status. In the American social structure, so far as division of labour is concerned, nationalities often take the place occupied by social classes in Europe; racial feeling to a certain extent takes the place of class prejudice. As "green-horns," the immigrants became "Wop labour," "Hunky labour," "Kike labour," "Dago labour," or another derisively branded section of foreign labour. Most of them had been peas-ants in their home countries, but even the highly skilled work-ers were compelled to abandon their former occupations in the attempt to fit themselves into the new economic life in America. These people, already infected with the pejorative moral qual-ity of being aliens, were conspicuous not only because of their physical appearance but also because of their extreme poverty, which forced them to seek refuge in the socially disorganized districts, the congested slums, the sordid haunts of deterioration and demoralization. Although their own hygienic notions were not in contrast to the conditions of their quarters, both sexes and all ages were crowded into quarters so small and ill equipped that sufficient privacy and conveniences for the development of ordinary standards of modesty and decency were beyond possibility. Not restrained by the social control of their traditional social environment, their moral standards had already suffered, and the conditions in which this unorganized mass had to live, the disreputable environment, and the disturbed balance of the sexes, made them grow "wild." Venereal diseases, juvenile delinquency, and crime spread.

All these circumstances only corroborated the already existing opinion about their inherent tendencies to squalor, crime, and vice: they were disorderly, ignorant, superstitious, inefficient, and filthy; they had anti-social habits. The society in which they intruded as actual or potential under-bidding competitors—thus representing a menace to the so-called "American standards of wages and of living"—had not invited them. Their invasion often meant an encroachment on the status of the people in whose district they settled. Contact increased dislike, bred intolerance. Dissimilarity inevitably provoked ill feeling. Unlikeness suggested inequality, which appealed to the consciousness of superiority on the part of the older residents. In the new environment the immigrants' helplessness, resulting from a realization of incongruities between themselves and American life, only made them the butt of jokes and sneers, if not of contempt and insult. Both they and the society had to build up attitudes of defence.

Self-defence on the part of American society was natural,

inevitable. These immigrants came in such overwhelming numbers that disintegration seemed to impend. Not only did they not conform to the American standard; they even endangered its perpetuation. As a result came the tendency to segregate them. The older settlers wanted to safeguard their own patterns of behaviour, which were constantly being threatened with submersion by the tide of the newcomers. Prejudice became the subconscious defence mechanism; racial theories, its rationalization; discrimination, sometimes sanctioned by legislation, its device for maintaining social distance, for preserving "Nordic supremacy."

The less moulded by history, the less organic, the more loosely composed and less integrated a society is, the stronger the prejudice, the less the reliance upon spontaneous social control, the more artificial the means resorted to in its struggle for perpetuation.

American society is still young. Built by but a few generations of vigorous pioneers with heterogeneous backgrounds, the social structure lacks the unifying memories and experiences of a common past, in which foundation the more mature nations are rooted. For this reason the largely unconscious fear of disintegration and the instinctive need for maintaining social identity becomes almost an obsession.

This uneasiness is also responsible for the popular concept of Americanization; it is urged by a public opinion which demands the elimination of unlikeness. It demands the unquestioning abandonment and absolute forgetfulness on the part of the immigrant of all obligations and connexions with other countries because of descent or birth, the suppression and repudiation of all signs that distinguish him from Americans. He should definitely slough off all foreign allegiance and affiliation and lose all trace or suggestion of his foreign origin. It seems unnecessary here to analyse how much in this "commandment" is due to the disenchantment caused by the experiences during the World War and how much is due to Puritanical reminiscences of Saint Paul's exhortation to put off the corrupt "old man." [1] Suffice to say that it is rooted in the yearning for unity and social security, and not only demands a rigid, unreserved self-effacement, but at the same time precludes the possibility of assimilation for those who are conspicuous by reason of colour or language. In fact it is a credo which is often paraphrased as the desire for preserving racial purity, a doctrine which is the more tenaciously and aggressively clung to the less it is amenable to the processes of logic. It has become part of the unquestioned and undiscussible *mores*.

This demand for uncompromising conformity to the pattern, rooted in the uneasiness resulting from the mass invasion by so many heterogeneous elements, grows into a passion for homogeneity and into its emotional derivative, intolerance. It explains the intense pressure towards uniformity symptomatic of the present American civilization, and the emphasis on a kind of standardized "loyalty" and canonized "patriotism." This attitude on the part of the dominant group is all but natural. The economic position of this group expresses itself in the social and cultural fields by setting the standards and the pattern to which—by social pressure, if not by actual compulsion—the weaker groups are urged to comply. These weaker groups are all too eager to comply. Indeed, the immigrant knows that, if he does not lose the marks of his identity, he will, in the American mind, permanently be associated with the mass of unskilled labourers which constitute his minority group. So the stimulus to imitation—to at least outward conformity—is very strong.

[1] Ephesians 4: 22; Colossians 3: 9–10; and Romans 6.

Under the perturbed conditions after the World War, when America's relative isolation was broken and new ideas and habits poured into the country, the tendency to self-preservation grew stronger still. A widespread distrust of all things foreign, a fear psychology, inspired the repudiation of Wilson's policies, the radical change in immigration policy, the glorification of the Nordic race as identified with the old American stock, the Americanization movement, and the modern Ku-Klux Klan. All these expressions of the desire to maintain "100 per cent Americanism" appealed strongly to the average man, not hampered by the need for critical analysis and reflection, satisfied with conventional stereotypes, and made uneasy by situations involving the integrity of the nation's life. He yearned for likemindedness—conformity.

The great concern which emphasized the demand for unity and uniformity was not due only to the ever-rising tide of heterogeneous immigrants; the instability of American life itself was at the root of these misgivings. American society was still in an unconsolidated state and was in transition at the time when the constant stream of newcomers flooded the country. In a relatively short time this country had developed from a simply organized, agricultural community into an elaborate, complicated, mechanical, and industrial society.

If towns of 8000 population are taken as the dividing line, less than 5 per cent of the people were urban in 1820, and only one employed person in five was engaged in non-agricultural pursuits. In 1849 the value of agricultural exports was still 81 per cent of the value of all exports; by 1925 the value of non-agricultural exports had grown to 52 per cent of the total. By 1900 the urban population had grown from 5 to 33 per cent and in 1920 to 44 per cent; the number of cities with a population of 8000 or more inhabitants had increased from 6 in 1790 to 924 in 1920. Between 1880 and 1920 those at work in agriculture had declined from 50 per cent of the total working population to 26 per cent, while the manufacturing and mechanical occupations had increased in the same period from 24 to 30 per cent and those in trade and transportation from 12 to 25 per cent. From 1910 to 1930 agricultural employment was reduced by 11 per cent; the numbers attached to mining rose 2 per cent, to manufacturing and mechanical pursuits 32 per cent, and to transportation 38 per cent. Employment in trade and in the combined professional services rose 75 and 80 per cent respectively. In 1920, 51.4 per cent and, in 1930, 56.2 per cent of the population of the nation was living in towns of 2500 or more inhabitants. According to Woofter's computation, 60.6 per cent of the population of 1930 must be classified as urban. One person in every three lived on farms in 1910, one in four in 1925, whereas in 1930 farms could claim hardly more than one person in five. Between 1820 and 1930 the proportion of those employed in agriculture to the total population ten years of age and over declined from 32.14 to 10.62 per cent, while the proportion of the population gainfully employed rose from 44.7 to 49.5 per cent. It has been estimated that between 1922 and 1929 there was a net average annual shift to the cities of nearly 800,000, consisting for a disproportionately large percentage of the young and of females, the most unstable elements in a society. This development was the result of the passing of agricultural self-sufficiency, the commercialization and mechanization of agriculture, the agricultural depression as an aftermath of the World War, and the rise and growth of the industries with their expanding demand for labour.

For those who moved into the cities there was the serious problem of effecting a shift in residence and of fitting into new lines of employment. Instead of working for themselves, they were faced with the uncertainty and the anxiety of earning a living from employment. The self-employed farmers and agricultural labourers and those members of the family who had before pursued their economic activities within their own homes shifted to the status of wage-earners and salary workers. There was a constant break-up of established relations, interests, and occupations, a continuous necessity for a more or less difficult readjustment. The growth of the railroads, the spread of the automobile, and the improvement of the highway system increased the mobility of the population.

The typical American city was persistently expanding. Because it was growing, its various utilization areas—its commercial districts, its residential sections, its industrial regions, and its dormitory suburbs—were constantly in movement, jostling one against the other, and disrupting each other's community life. The development of rapid-transit facilities made available for residential and commercial utilization areas that had hitherto been relatively inaccessible.

The constant stream from the rural areas to the cities not only brought a sweeping metamorphosis of physical conditions, but also caused a state of ever-increasing social disorganization. With the rapid growth of the cities, the intrusion into residential communities by business and industry effected a disintegration of the community as a unit of social control. The multiplicity of contacts and the diversity of the codes of conduct brought about the liberation of the individual from traditional ways of thinking and behaviour.

The phenomenon in itself was not new to America. The immigrant—as was already stated above—had freed himself from the traditional social control of his home community, and in the sparsely populated territories of pioneer America he found ample opportunity for self-development not hampered by social and governmental constraint. But social life is a continuously renewed effort of the group to readjust its relationships, to reintegrate its identity. So, as years passed, relationships were established among these immigrants; social life evolved, growing into a new society with its own *mores*.

That society was now, as a result of the economic innovation, threatened with the break-down of the existing social codes. This again freed the individual, who migrated to the cities from the social restraints imposed by living in an ordered community.

This individual freedom is not a clear gain, however stimulating it may be to "progress." Diminished social control demands an accession of intelligent self-control and understanding, which are relatively rare. When the social organization disintegrates, there are withdrawn the social support and discipline so necessary to most people. Individuals lack the great feeling of "belonging," and in the promiscuity of city life they are unable to formulate for themselves substitute standards, attitudes, and habits. Impulses and wishes take random and wild expression. Freed from all intimate social relationships and perhaps moving and living in widely separated and conflicting worlds, many people lose their personality, their personal equilibrium, are abandoned to a disordered isolation, and become demoralized. They may lose that for which they previously were valued, their technical skill, which was the basis of their self-esteem but which in the new environment is no longer of use. From the social void about them, psychoneurosis, political extremism, delinquency, criminality, and suicide shoot up like mushrooms. Crime statistics show that these symptoms of gross social disorganization and individual maladjustment have not been lacking in the cities into which the migrating rural population crowded.

Moreover, the new freedom has subjected the individual to business, and employment opportunities are now more limited than in the days of vast unclaimed resources and a beckoning frontier. When times are good, he may lose his job through technical changes or because of his age. In a period of depression he may be laid off and at the same time be prevented from seeking another occupation because of the closing down of other places of employment. The swift and universal changes in industry require constant adjustments by the workers. Any considerable and sustained interruption in their money income exposes them to hardships which they were in a better position to mitigate when they were members of an agricultural or rural community. These changes in industry assumed an almost revolutionary character during the decade of the 1920's. In the railroad industry, for instance, the decline in employment from all causes between 1920 and 1930 amounted to the displacement of some 535,000 workers, many of whom, in the process of finding new jobs, were bound to suffer considerable periods of unemployment. Changes in the location of industries or employment of a cheaper type of labour have the same effect. This economic insecurity has created a mood of restless uneasiness to which the job impersonality in large offices and industrial units also contributed.

The break-down of ordered community life as a consequence of this overwhelming and disorderly expansion brought about weakening of control by the *mores* over the members of the community. Social change resulted in social unrest. Adaptation to the new situation was the more difficult since, because of the constant shifting of occupation and residence, there was no stability. The "unlimited possibilities" caused a planless, restless, and endless pursuit—with happiness always lying beyond any present achievement.

In a way this is the tragic plight of the whole modern civilization. For "progress" we pay the price of dissatisfaction. Disturbance of communal integrity is everywhere a concomitant of rapid economic growth. But in America this general tendency is stronger than in the older nations because these nations—with their homogeneous populations and older traditions—have better preserved their unity of life, their social integrity, and their social code. They are therefore more resistant to sudden change, whereas the glorification of individualism is part of the American *mores*.

Social disruption is general. The new apartment life restricts the importance of what formerly was regarded as the essential function of the family. Husband and wife [2] often work at a great distance from their home and must travel several hours every day. In a residential neighbourhood not far from New York, it was found that each five years over 78 per cent of its population moved to a new address. Under these circumstances the education of the children has also become a problem which some wish to solve by substituting the school for the parents.

Mobility is typical of urban life. In the rooming-house areas of the cities the average residence term of the occupants does not exceed four months. The instability of the different urban sections becomes the nightmare of the conservative citizen who has invested his savings in real estate but must shift again and again lest what yesterday seemed valuable property be worthless tomorrow. The impulse to own one's own home fades away. In the hotels and apartment houses people live in physical nearness, but the social distances are enormous. People live side by side but are not neighbours. They do not even realize the divergence of each other's interests and backgrounds; they simply do not know each other. Life is adventurous but often so very lonely.

Civic societies, churches, Y.M.C.A.'s, and the like try to make up for this general lack of stability, which is an impedi-

---

[2] In 1930 the number of working women constituted 22.1 per cent of the total female population ten years of age and over.

ment to the transformation of the chaos into a new collective organism, to the establishment of new social forms of living, to the reintegration of society. For perpetual migration removes the people from active participation in a common social life and communal responsibility. The result is, on the one hand, that the groups that have survived or have gradually developed jealously keep together to preserve their integrity; on the other hand, there is that pressure towards uniformity, indicative of the desperate struggle for a new level at which coherence and social collaboration will again be possible.

In this state of disorganization of American society—as a consequence of the swift and continuing evolution of industry and its aftermath, the exodus from the rural communities to the hastily expanding cities—in this general state of social and communal disintegration, the stupendous injection of foreign elements brought additional confusion. Thus the prevailing fear of the loss of identity amid all the turmoil is not surprising. Some of these misgivings were caused by the problem of the franchise for the new citizens belonging to the "new immigration." Had they already sufficiently imbibed the spirit of "American democracy"? Was the future of American institutions sufficiently guaranteed in the hands of these voters, or would these newly made citizens be led by their loyalty to a foreign power and perhaps even be an easy prey to foreign machinations? This, however, was only rationalization. The reality was that the politicians were only too eager to win these additional votes which were easily bought by cash or favours. Both major political parties sinned, but it is always the party to which we do not belong that is to blame. Then apprehension rose again when great numbers of Jewish, Irish, and Italian immigrants finally did become voters and effectively could and did influence politics. In the turmoil of partisan politics people could not see that, at the same time, the political influence of these new Americans was growing more worthy. People noticed only the sordid practices of the ward politician and the egotism of the business man or self-made man who used public office for his own purposes or ambitions. They did not notice the small but growing number that gradually were beginning to feel the sense of civic responsibility and the obligation to serve. Therefore, participation in politics by these new citizens gave a fresh stimulus and a welcome justification to fixated opinion about their less desirable qualities. Politics, and especially American politics, open the way to practices which are condemned in ordinary life. Is it not that unalloyed American and democrat, Andrew Jackson, whose name will always be associated with the triumph of the spoils system in national politics? It is very difficult for an outsider with divergent standards and traditions to make an evaluation of the comparative political morality of the different nationalities which constitute the American nation—the good old stock not excluded.

There were additional reasons for anxiety. In New England —not long ago the typical habitat of the pure old American stock, an area with well-defined social classes and established traditions—there are now, as a result of the industrial development, several hundred thousands of French-Canadians. Wherever these have settled in numbers, that community is gradually ceasing to be English. Lewiston, Maine, is an example. It not only has ceased to be a Yankee city and is losing its American characteristics, but it is gradually assuming a French aspect. The parish with its organizations has successfully prevented its parishioners from coming under native influences and is driving the English language from the business sections. The French-Canadians of Biddeford, Maine, constitute over 70 per cent of the total population. This nationality is fairly well distributed over the whole city. A Yankee section exists, rather than a French section. The Canadians, although Roman Catholics, do not mix even with the Irish.

For the cities the foreign-born element is indeed enormous. In only twenty-eight of the sixty-eight cities having more than 100,000 inhabitants in 1920 did native whites of native parentage constitute as much as one-half of the population. In nineteen of these cities, sixteen of which were in the New England and Middle Atlantic states, over two-thirds of the population consisted of foreign-born whites and their children. In twenty-one of them, including New Bedford (40 per cent), New York (35 per cent), Chicago (30 per cent), and Boston (32 per cent), the foreign-born alone constituted more than one-fourth of the population.

In this way American society—by a universal lack of natural, spontaneous participation on terms of unconscious fellowship in the manifold activities of a common social life—seems to constitute a loose agglomeration, a mere symbiosis, of many diverse, deeply entrenched, incompatible, and mutually exclusive nationalities separated from each other by the virtually insuperable barriers of an intense particularism. If the spheres in which these nationalities move should grow more and more distinct and irreconcilable, what would be the end?

This separatism was evident not only between the different nationalities; it was characteristic of the disorganized society as a whole. All the groups that had preserved their integrated character during the industrial revolution, or newly had crystallized from the chaos, or were struggling to build up a new solidarity were defending their identities by a certain degree of segregation. A patent evidence of the uneasiness caused by the invasion of newcomers and resulting in an attitude of self-protection was displayed by the Negroes in Chicago. When the stream of southern Negroes poured into their section, the older Negro settlers, who had developed a certain degree of consciousness of solidarity, of like-mindedness, and of common feeling, and who had built up certain standards of conduct and a scheme of life of their own, viewed the influx of the immigrants with suspicion and alarm. They feared the social anarchy that inevitably would result from the inroads of these unattached elements upon the consistency and integrity of their group life, and guarded the homogeneous character of their group very jealously, especially since the incursion of these southern Negroes endangered their status. The desire for social security made them move out to other districts, where they in turn encountered the same apprehension on the part of the white residents there.

The same process that upset the organization of the established Negro community of Chicago manifested itself wherever there was industrial development. The foreign immigrants, of course, formed only an additional complicating element in the general unrest of American society in its unconscious struggle to re-establish communal life. In the cities a constant process of distribution was going on, which sifted and allocated individuals and groups by nationality and occupations. Personal tastes and convenience, vocational and economic interests, infallibly tended to segregate and thus to classify the population. In the course of time every section and quarter of the city took on something of the character and the qualities of its inhabitants. There were the business and industrial sections, the transition area, the rooming-house areas, the foreign sections, the zone of workingmen's homes, the areas of second and third settlement, the lower-middle-class districts, the upper-middle-class neighbourhoods, the exclusive residential sections. These demarcations in the mobility of American life were the visible proof of the inevitable appearance of a class society in America. Indeed, social equality is now a thing of

the past, although in the ecstatic phraseology of wishful thinking about "American democracy" this is not admitted, or
rather, its consequences are evaded: not "everybody," not even
"anybody" a king.

The stirring principles of the Declaration of Independence
—the sacred trust of which the American nation is the custodian
and thus a missionary for the elevation of humanity—constitute
the distinctive ideology of an early pioneer life in a land of
opportunity, of a fierce frontier democracy of the Andrew
Jackson type in a period of expansion, and of a plain farmer
community in a day of self-sufficiency. So long as there was a
zone of free land on the western border of the settled area of
the United States, nobody was forced to accept a permanent
position of social subordination in the class societies of the eastern seaboard states, or of the Gulf states when after 1800 the
spread of cotton culture had given rise to the great plantations.
But the disappearance of the frontier closed the gate of escape.
The increased density of the population and the sweeping industrial development have made society so complicated that
a stratification was bound to result from it.

In the same way the concept of liberty has fundamentally
changed. The motives that drove the Armenians, the Poles,
the Jews, and the Irish to America were no less respectable
than those of the Pilgrim fathers, Huguenots, or the early
Pennsylvania Dutch. However, since "zealous watchfulness"
in guarding "the people's interests" put in force the restrictions
of the Immigration Act of 1924, the United States is no longer
"the home for the persecuted," the traditional "haven of refuge" for the downtrodden and oppressed of any and all countries. Since 1900 European radicals have not had the right
of political asylum in the United States. And what about the
freedom of thought, speech, and assembly which once seemed
fundamental in the American system? Especially since 1917

have the concept and practice of these historic civil liberties, even in the restricted form of "academic freedom" in the universities, remained untouched? It was impossible in a society which irresistibly tended towards accumulation of capital and concentration of power; combination of business enterprise and centralization of business control, monopoly and oligarchy, mechanization and standardization, all serving to promote uniformity. Nevertheless, the sacred myth of liberty and equality is still the national confession of faith and an incentive to indomitable optimism. This explains the unwillingness to recognize such effects of social evolution as the stratification of society.

That class distinction exists was already apparent from what was said above about the reaction of the older Negro settlers in Chicago to the invasion of the southern Negroes. We find it reflected also in the flight of the German Jews from the Russian Jews and in the separatist existence of the "Jewish Mayflower stock," the Spanish-Portuguese Jewish *élite* in New York City. Not so long ago marriage with the Ashkenazim was frowned upon by the Sephardic Jews. Similar instances of class consciousness can be quoted about the native American community. The closed-door policy of exclusive private schools and the snobbishness of some elect fraternities and sororities are examples; the interest certain "Dames" and "Daughters" display in their ancestry is another. There is in the big cities the exclusive, highly class-conscious "society" composed of the "socially acceptable" whose names are recorded in the "Social Register" and who play the "social game." There are the "climbers" who struggle to break into the circles of those who are "in." But because of the mobility of the population, class demarcations are not yet distinctly drawn although several strata already are emerging. The mobility of American labour and the individualism in the *mores* still impede the consolidation of real class consciousness on the part of the workingmen.

As compared with the large cities, the smaller cities in the country (about 30,000 inhabitants), which were not so much affected by the industrial change and the invasion from the rural districts, display a more stabilized character. There the outstanding social cleavage—roughly speaking—is constituted by a division into a lower and a higher middle class, or a business class and a working class. The latter addresses its activities in getting its living primarily to *things*, utilizing material tools in the making of things and the performance of services. The members of the other group address their activities predominantly to *people* in the selling or promotion of things, services, and ideas. The mere fact of being born into the one group or the other is the most significant single cultural factor tending to influence what one does all day long throughout one's life, whom one marries, when one gets up in the morning, whether one belongs to the Holy Roller or Presbyterian church, whether one drives a Ford or a Buick, whether one sits about evenings with one's necktie on or off, whether one belongs to the Masonic Order or not. In the older cities of the East, especially on the Atlantic seaboard in South Carolina and in old New England, the social tissue is far more elaborate. In some cases five to seven distinct social classes exist, all moving in separate circles, with their peculiar tasks and functions, their privileges and their prejudices.

Class differentiations have become an integral feature of American life. The employee, or wage-earning, class is a distinct and separate element in the population. While there is a theoretical possibility, and not infrequently actual examples, of moving up out of this class, the feasibility or likelihood of such an outcome is becoming so slight as to exercise less and less influence on the general situation.

For our purpose, however, it is more important to investi-

gate what role is attributed to the nationalities in the effort
to harmonize the discrepancy between the social reality and the
traditional ideology. "Unconscious class consciousness" per-
meates the whole society. Nationalities are so often blamed for
attitudes which are objectionable only because of the existence
of class distinction. Armenians and Jews, for instance, have the
reputation of being very "obtrusive." If we enter into the
merits of this case, however, it appears that this reputation is
due more particularly to the behaviour of some get-rich-quick
Armenians and Jews. This is easily explained. All over the
world people who attain a new status suddenly—an influential
position, wealth, or freedom—are prone to become conceited
and inconsiderate of others. Immigrants who advance in this
country are no exception in their endeavour to "keep up with
the Joneses." They are likely to display these characteristics
even in an exaggerated form, as the natural social restraints are
lacking. Moreover, aggressiveness is also the ordinary reaction
of the suppressed individual who tries to make up for his inferiority. Boasting and loud talk are other forms of the same
reaction. What elsewhere is considered as the typical attitude
of the newly rich is here attributed to certain nationalities,
some members of which—in conformity with the American
spirit of "getting ahead"—have been successful in accumulat-
ing wealth. The culturally dominant race, shocked by the
"airs" these people assume, fears being "overrun"; it believes
that the status and "rights" of the American "class" are being
jeopardized. In this manner the social reality is interpreted
not in terms of a differentiation in classes but in terms of an
antithesis between Americans and the intruding immigrant
nationalities, against whose "un-American" ways the Americans
must uphold the heritage of the fathers. People are looked
down upon not because they are considered to belong to a
lower class but because of their imputed inferior cultural status

—they are not up to the American standard. By the use of this stereotype the ideology remains untouched.

Actually, however, nationalities play the role of classes in the American social structure. So certain nationalities can also mount to a higher economic and social level if other nationalities take their place below. This change is usually accompanied by a removal to better residences, the successors to their work and status moving into the vacated living quarters. There was a time when the bulk of the Irish formed the pick-and-shovel caste, claiming exclusive possession of the poorest and least honourable occupations and mobbing the Chinese or the Negro who intruded. The Italians and some of the nationalities of eastern Europe now wield the shovel, and the Irish have escaped their competition by running nimbly up the ladder of occupations.

Nowadays the work classifies the nationality. For instance, it is observed that soon after Slavic labour invades a steel mill, the native American labour leaves altogether because of the stigma impressed on that type of work by the employment of immigrants. However, invasion is difficult; it meets with passionate resistance, for status is involved. Moved by the desire and necessity for adjustments in costs, industry nevertheless is constantly seeking new sources of cheaper labour; when it has found them, it proceeds with the task of replacing one type with another. This has been a continuous process in which first one and then another of the available supplies of labour have been tapped. Sometimes economic compulsion can urge a class of people to take up work that was formerly despised as the typical work of a lower class. In that case energy is concentrated upon the wholesale expulsion of that lower class from its traditional occupation in order to remove the stigma. This was the plight of the Chinese when organized white labour succeeded in finally displacing them in California. In this way class prejudice is dissolved in race prejudice. This means that for the "forgotten man" the opportunity to rise is more limited than in a modern (non-feudal) class society; the fixation of status of the different social groups on the basis of nationality, priority, and characteristic occupations has the tendency to immobilize the social structure into a caste system. Neither the traditional worship of success—the old democratic admiration for the self-made man and the deference to the rights of competitive individual development—nor the newer philosophy of "the economy of high wages" are consistent with the demand that the under-privileged groups keep in their places.

This situation makes accommodation on the part of the immigrants the more difficult. They feel themselves discriminated against and exploited; sometimes they are inspired with hatred against the Land of (broken) Promise. This lack of adjustment also makes them susceptible to radical and extremist agitation. The fomenters of "Red scares," however, interpret this phenomenon as an evidence of the alien's undesirability; he is accused of importing and spreading un-American doctrines—a new justification for the fixated prejudice.

As natural as the struggle on the part of American society to preserve the endangered integrity of its group life and to regain the ability to act corporately was the need of the immigrant nationalities for protecting their identities. This protection was found in the acceptance of the enforced isolation into self-respecting ghettoes and other homogeneous "racial" colonies which tended to maintain the folkways of the old country and helped the unstable newcomers to preserve their sense of social responsibility. These colonies, of course, retard the assimilation process, but by saving the immigrants from demoralization they serve a useful purpose. Many immigrants became conscious of their nationality only after they had entered America. Between 1890 and 1910 these foreign colonies doubled and trebled their numbers. Immigrant community life grew. The massing together in a more or less limited area of like-minded individuals heightened group consciousness. Common needs in the new environment, the prejudice of the outside world, the common tie of nationality, the neighbour-hood spirit, and class interests moulded them into a solidary group. There was even a tendency for these groups to grow economically more and more self-sufficient, of course within clearly definable limits.

From the standpoint of organization the foreign colony is far more vital than any of the groupings in the modern city society. There are the personal relations, the direct participa-tion in community life, the solidarity, the interdependence, in-teraction, intercommunication characteristic of the primary group. There is the intimacy which unconsciously regulates the individual behaviour according to the *mores*. The foreign col-ony is held together in one social psychologic process.

The groupings in the great society of the city are far more loosely composed. The municipal goverment does not repre-sent the community, as there is no community. Municipal legislation is passed for the city as a whole, but embodies the values of the more homogeneous and stable, respectable out-lying residential areas where the standards are based on the social situation of yesterday. Here people are periodically star-tled by dramatic accounts of vice and crime. Not feeling the need for studying what is at the basis of these accounts or simply unwilling to face the socially conditioned reality, public opin-ion resolves that something must be done. Then attempts are made to fix certain limits to individuation of behaviour and to urge compliance with certain standards; legislation is enacted which the police are supposed to enforce. Here again the public does not face the reality of American democracy, which has

subjected police to politics and inevitably made politicians depend upon the disorderly elements that originate the vice and
crime. This situation determines how far law enforcement
goes. So it appears that democracy is more realistic than the
standards according to which it tries to regulate itself.

Modern society is not a community but consists of groupings. There are, in the first place, the interest groups, such as
the trade unions and the employer organizations, but there is
no personal interrelationship of a sentimental order. The
same holds true of various associations for good government.
The occupation, the vocation, the profession, and the calling
may each select and develop a certain type of predisposition
and mould its people—the shopgirl, the policeman, the taxi
driver, the tailor, the teacher, the lawyer, the doctor, the minister. Although this is likely to evolve a certain occupational
code of honour and a certain weak form of solidarity, there
are no sentimental ties which bind the representatives of these
occupations together into an organic unity.

A certain degree of unity is attained by the agencies for
shaping public opinion and common attitudes. These may
sometimes lead to collective action, but not to collective behaviour and corporate action in the full sense of these words.
These agencies are the press, the advertising agencies, the
radio, and the movies. They serve to create standardized desires; they give opportunity for "identification," "projection,"
and participation but—it seems a paradox—in an impersonal
way; they tend towards indoctrination and inculcation, but only
in so far as they build on existing common fears, latent opinions, real or imaginary needs. However rationalized their purpose may be, these agencies offer, *must* offer, their material in
such a way as to appeal to the emotions. Their effectiveness
depends on a scientific or intuitive knowledge of human nature
of the kind displayed by the labour agitator, the Salvation

Army leader, the revivalist, and the political speaker, who know how to transform a crowd into an organized drive. They take advantage of the unstable equilibrium of city society with its strong emotional trend which feeds on thrill and therefore is sensitive to sudden alarm and every new wind of doctrine. By publicity these agencies effect a certain social control and by presenting complicated problems in the simplified, condensed, and vivified form of slogans, symbols, stereotypes, and cartoons they produce some sort of working democracy and regulate conduct. They teach what to eat or drink, how to behave, how to be amused. They are the agencies for bringing about uniformity.

More personal, and consequently deeper, is the influence of the political machine, which appeals not only to some vague or more conscious need, but also to the vital desire for security, contact, and guidance.

As a gregarious animal, the individual in the city still has the basic desire for response, for recognition, and for support. These desires can be satisfied only by associating with a group of like-minded comrades. Gangs, night-clubs, art circles, recreation centres, and sport centres may provide for such association. However, it makes a great deal of difference whether these centres are created by the city, or by the corporation of which one is the employee, or by an organization to which one belongs and which gives the "we-feeling" and stimulates self-pride. Clubs, shrines, lodges, fraternal orders, and civic societies—even if the relations between the members as a whole often may be of a more or less impersonal nature—tend to produce this feeling, as do the social circle (the "society," the clique) and the neighbourhood, although the latter is no longer "the village within the city." Special mention should be given the community organized around the neighbourhood school. But most important in this connexion is the function of the churches, which by selection of their membership from distinct social classes and by their social and recreational activities serve to form groups and to develop group life; but city churches also have their struggle with the mobility of the population, and the drifting younger generation of the furnished rooms turns its back on them.

Finally, the established residential neighbourhoods, in which the more settled type of population resides, with their comparative preponderance of women and children, serve as the custodians of the stabilizing and repressive folkways. These conservative, law-abiding, civic-minded people form the dominant group that sets the pattern and the standards for imitation. They display a certain economic and cultural homogeneity and maintain their stability by attracting appropriate elements and repelling incongruous, less responsible, and undesirable "invaders." But in none of these groups are the relationships so close, so inclusive, and so intimate as in the immigrant colony, even where there is a distinction of classes within the colony. This is the reason underlying the fear of the unassimilability of the foreign colonies.

If we compare the Oriental immigration on the West Coast with the "new immigration" in the East, the resemblances are striking. All the objectionable features quoted as proof of the undesirability and unassimilability of the Orientals have their parallels in the history of the new immigration. In both cases we find the foreign colony, even the area of second settlement, and the difficulty encountered by the under-privileged in moving to the better residential districts. The quaint appearance of the Chinese has its equivalent in that of the Eastern Jews; the Japanese "picture-bride" corresponds to a similar custom among the Polish immigrants; the Chinese aversion for making America a permanent home is found among other immigrant groups, notably the Italians and the Poles. Peonage and sweat-shop practices, with which the Chinese and Japanese immigrants were charged, are not uncommon among the Greek, south Italian, and Jewish immigrants. The inferior status of the women is by no means an Oriental monopoly. The birth-rate of the Italians is not less than that of the Japanese which frightened California. There are Italian communities that stick far more jealously to the customs and habits of their native villages in Sicily and elsewhere than the Chinese ever have done to theirs. The same holds true for some Jewish settlements in New York. With the same pathetic ingenuity as the Japanese, the older generation of other immigrant groups, in a vain search for their lost children, have attempted to reclaim those who have strayed away, to prevent the growing youth from falling a prey to the same alienating influences, and to preserve the delicate network of precious traditions, cultural values, and ideals which is being ruthlessly torn asunder. The language schools of California have their counterpart in similar institutions of the old and new immigrations, even as far as their objectives are concerned. The Japanese associations of America can be compared with similar nationalistic organizations of the Italians, the Hungarians, and the Poles. Criminal Chinese secret societies find their match in the Italians' Black Hand organizations; police and press find both inevitable and hopeless of destruction. Like Japan, Italy has been particularly active in preserving the allegiance of her emigrated subjects. As for the unsanitary conditions and unhygienic habits of Chinatown, they are by no means unique!

Nevertheless, as generations pass, these solitary segregated distinct immigrant communities, however inaccessible and unassimilable they may seem, however obstinate the prejudice against them may be, and however shaky the basis for conciliation and harmony may appear, will dissolve and change. This will come about largely through the public school, which is one point at which contact with American life is inevitable, and more particularly through the education the children give each other. The moment the child crosses the threshold of the school house, the question of his future fealty is settled. It is futile to argue with a youthful head to which nothing appeals more convincingly than physical greatness: a rich republic almost as large as all Europe put together, with 123,000,000 inhabitants, with rivers like the Mississippi, with two oceans, with one of the two largest cities in the world, and so on, and on.

The "diluted" second generation is the fatal disease gnawing at the vitals of particularism. The sophisticated immigrant, who often has *his* feeling of superiority, may grow sceptical about the sublimity of democracy and the equality of all before the bar of American justice. He may see how votes are openly bought by cash or favours; political graft is taken for granted; gangs are protected, financed, and organized by politicians as a tool in building up their own or local political machines; false canvasses of the vote are made; election officials and voters are intimidated and terrorized; and justice lends a ready ear to the ward boss or even to the precinct captain. But the member of the second generation knows how to play the game himself. At the same time, unconscious of any inconsistency, he can indulge in passionate oratory, consisting of a glorification of the lofty qualities of American democracy, for he has already assimilated Babbitt's unreflective conventional loyalty, ecstatic vocabulary, and specious humanitarianism.

The simple immigrant may live for years in the colony of which he is so integrally a part that he is unaware of its existence, but the children discover its foreignness for the parents. They go to school, work in stores and offices, make friends, go to dances; they are mobile, and the colony world begins to shrink, to bore, and finally to disgust. Trying to live in two social worlds, the youngsters find it impossible to conform in both at the same time. They also feel the loss of status attached to their connexion with the colony. They grow out of patience with the petty interests and quarrels of the older group, and finally refuse to have their lives ordered by their parents, whom they know to be ignorant and inexperienced. Sometimes parents who feel at home because they have never been outside resist for some time; then family conflicts arise that make life intolerable. They eventually yield, and the exodus begins. Families are not being broken up; the deep affections persist. Though the old folks still may have misgivings, in their indulgent way they are letting the new generation take the lead and are proud of their progressive sons and daughters.

Americanization works unconsciously. Time is the great assimilator. The once strong prejudice against the Germans and the Irish, who were not so long ago regarded with disdain and even hatred, has largely disappeared, since their economic status has improved. They have lost their visibility, not only in outward appearance but also in their habits, speech, and outlook on life; they conform to the conventional pattern: they have learned how to "get on."

The same is true for the "new immigration." As their Americanization progresses, the immigrants move successively from the transition area to the areas of second and third settlement, which mark different phases in a process of gradual adaptation to the requirements of the American environment. "To move uptown" is the dearest dream of the progressive immigrant family of New York, and that desire urges towards conformity. The rise in economic status, encouraging greater mobility, tends to split the original nucleus. The more well-to-do individuals and families move out of the congested area to reside in sections where they find themselves a minority among other minorities and where the characteristic landmarks of each immigrant colony are no more to be found. Financial success on the part of the enterprising immigrant means a severance of ties with his less fortunate brethren, who are left behind to struggle alone. In the wider, freer world of anonymity which he enters, a powerful, invisible, irresistible steam roller ruthlessly irons out the differences. In this way the successful individual matriculates into the American community. "Individual enterprise" is not only the way out of the particularism of the nationality and the way to the great society; it is also indicative of the immigrant's absorption by the prevailing philosophy.

Besides, from a psychic point of view, Americans and the members of these immigrant groups are all identical in this respect: both belong to the "immigrant-type." This implies that, although they may differ in temperamental disposition, they have, to a certain extent and perhaps in a varied degree, the same distinctive traits in common, the same predominant attitudes. Owing to the selection process of immigration, they represent the same variety of *Homo sapiens*. These identical psychic characteristics cannot fail to facilitate that mutual understanding which is the basis for a future *rapprochement*.

The difference between the Oriental and the "new immigration" is that, although neither the Chinese nor the Japanese have displayed anything like the resistance to assimilation shown by the Poles, they retain their distinctive biological features, however Americanized they may have become. This visibility, to which the prejudice has attached itself, keeps alive and persistently irritates the emotional associations connected with these physical characteristics. Since the *mores* have a tremendous inertia, these physical features—especially colour —will be the greatest obstacle to the social incorporation of these groups. For the Mexicans there is the language handicap, which is, apart from the slight colour barrier, the most concrete sign of unlikeness, the foremost object of animosity. Colour and language still seem practically irreconcilable with the axiomatic American conception of unification.

Another difference is that the concept of Japan is far more vivid and real to the Californians than that of Italy is to the population of the East. The attitude towards the Orientals on the West Coast and the attitude towards representatives of the new immigration in other parts of the country may be basically the same; on the other hand, it cannot be denied that the reaction of the Pacific Coast has been much more vehement than elsewhere. This difference in attitude can be explained largely by the fact that, at the time of the first Oriental immigration, American society in California was but a loose aggregation of recently arrived immigrants from all parts of America and elsewhere, whereas in the East group life was already more settled. In other words social disorganization was greater in California than in the East. The consternation of the gold-rush period combined with the bitter memories of the subsequent decades is responsible for the anti-Oriental tradition of the Pacific Coast and has left an almost ineradicable complex of collective antipathy in the *mores* of California. That antipathy has attached itself to colour.

The South and the Negro

AFTER our outline of the Chinese, Japanese, Mexican, and Indian situations and our analysis of certain aspects of the American attitude in interracial relations, it would be easy to make a summary of those traits which apply to the position of the Negro as well. However, such a compilation would not do justice to the specific conditions of the South. In many respects these conditions differ fundamentally from those discussed in previous chapters. Southern social life has not been disturbed by the intrusion of heterogeneous immigrant masses. Although there has been "a remarkable industrial development" in a limited area,[1] and several cities have shown a rapid growth, the South has remained predominantly agricultural. There is no spectre of Japan, no language trouble; the Negro has retained no civilization and no religion of his own. In order to understand the situation, it is necessary to look into the regional history. No interpretation of contemporary tendencies in the South would be adequate without some consideration of the past, the past to which the South looks back with a pathological nostalgia. That past, of course, culminated in the Civil War.

At the time of the war, the South, which had been ardently democratic in 1776, had slowly grown into the most complete aristocracy the United States has ever had. A few thousand great slave-owners scattered about the black belt from Rich-

[1] In the Piedmont from Danville, Virginia, to Birmingham, Alabama.

mond, Virginia, to Austin, Texas, received the bulk of the net returns from cotton, rice, and sugar plantations, and controlled every local legislature. They also nearly always managed to defeat their opponents in the race for Congress. The dominating position of this oligarchy can be likened only to that of the old coastwise aristocracy, which in the Southeast had controlled church, state, court, and lands, and which in New England between 1800 and 1820 took great alarm at the growing democratic influence in the interior.

The Civil War destroyed altogether the position of the Southern oligarchy. Many patricians had died on the battlefield; their great mansions had been pillaged and burned; the slaves had vanished; their live-stock had gone; their money had been lost in the annulment of the debts of the Confederacy; their land had deteriorated. The economic predominance of the ruling class had been practically annihilated in the debacle.

Even now it is still possible to form an impression of what the war meant to the South if one visits the old homes in Charleston—being shown around, after one has paid the entrance fees, by nervous old ladies who struggle to keep up the role of hostesses—and particularly if one tries to get a glimpse of the once prosperous plantation section. Of course, since the old days, hurricanes have devastated the area; the thriving rice culture has yielded to competition; the famous sea-island cotton has been infested by the boll-weevil. But the homes! Here the sad remains of an elaborate gateway, there a lonely drive of old oaks, there the broken pillars of a mansion portico, there bricks scattered in the dense shrubbery, yonder the wing of a manorial ruin remind one of vanished glories. Some of the ruins have been rebuilt by Northerners, but to the dreamer who seeks to enjoy undisturbed the greatness of the past and to those who can never forget, Yankee beautification is more odious than the decay of a unique splendour. The rice fields have turned into swamps; the pines have invaded the green pastures. On the estates some Negroes, descendants of the former slaves, are the guardians of the bygone age. The wreckage of homes and fields indicates where General Sherman passed. Indeed, the Civil War has left a trauma in the Southern soul.

The existing social order was shattered like the material culture. The whole complex of southern institutions had depended on the subordination of the Negro. With slavery destroyed, the labour system which had been the basis of the southern community was destroyed with it.

Under those chaotic conditions, the planters, who were without funds, without credit, and without dependable labour, moved into the towns. Here they found other whites, ruined and defiant like themselves; in the common distress they were in need of each other's sympathy. Here they could recall the days of yore and the exploits during the war, curse the Yankees who had disturbed a harmonious situation, discuss their overwhelming problems, build up a common defence attitude against the Negro, resolve to resist further federal interference, and brood on the restoration of white supremacy. Their consciousness of defeat gave rise to the compensatory mechanisms of self-praise and sectional pride; the North might have had—and still has—the brute force, but the South was superior in culture and refinement. This sublimation of the feeling of inferiority made them erect in every southern country town those pathetic monuments in honour of themselves denouncing the "unconstitutional attack."

Although materially in a prostrate condition, the old ruling class struggled to retain its leadership. However, the only claim to hegemony was the past. The present was dark; so was the future. The "aristocrats" thus sought the spiritual solace of retreat to a refuge secure against the doubtful implications of their position in post-bellum society; by way of psychological compensation, they idealized the superiority of the Old South —*their* civilization. "The world has never seen the equal of those days; nor in all the tides of time is it likely to do so again."

THE GREAT LEGEND

The sentimental stereotype of the great vanished culture became fixated: the grandeur and dignity of the century-old manorial mansion on a wooded hill near the river bank, its wide porch and great white Doric columns, spacious halls, and luxurious rooms, the distinction of its approach through stately avenues of live oaks draped in Spanish moss, the exquisite beauty of its landscaped garden, the extent of its rice and cotton fields limited only by blue horizon walls; the profusion of the Old South's proverbial hospitality, the medieval splendour and unalloyed mirth of its recreational life, the knightly magnificence and feudal providence of the refined but imperious and proud southern gentleman with his cavalier pedigree and his sensitive code of honour, the fragile loveliness and ravishing charm of the southern belle in hoop skirts; the solid satisfaction and loyal allegiance of the carefree, devoted slaves, including the affectionate, superstitious old mammy and the cheerful, humorous but irresponsible butler with his vanity over the standing of his "quality folks." All these traits were elaborated and recited world without end to glorify the superior social order of the past—the embodiment of the Golden Age.

Of course, there was some truth in the evasive idealism of the canonized tradition; it suffered only from a quantitative exaggeration and the inaccuracy of the suggested prevalence of a somewhat ideal type. In a few limited localities something approaching this order had existed: in tidewater Virginia, in the rice districts of coastal South Carolina, in the lower Mississippi Valley, and to a smaller extent in certain Piedmont sections. There had been, in reasonably large numbers, houses of comfort, and there had been a few homes of great beauty. Much of the power of personality which marked southern leadership was based on the confidence that comes from wide, if not profound, knowledge. No doubt there was an erudite *élite,* however small in number. Even now, courtesy of manner, courtliness of address towards women, patronizing kindness towards inferiors, delicacy in style of conversation, innate dignity, and cultured grace are still the distinction of the southern patrician of the older generation. Above all there was culture in the squirearchy; there was style that expressed itself in an art of living which did not dissolve into arts of nervous escape. Serenity and self-sufficiency, not dependent upon successful acquisition or accomplishment, were dominant traits which could flourish in a social order more interested in being than in becoming. Free from the restless urge towards more and still more attainment and material industriousness, this order developed a natural aptitude for taking time. Life was not broken up into two contrasting entities, unremitting toil and pleasure-seeking; its integrity was characterized by a leisurely dignity. This composed, self-contained state of mind enabled people equally to enjoy the eventful and the uneventful times. In that restrained, poised way of life speech was cultivated, conversation became an art, the conception of food and drink an ornament, the social ritual a quiet grace. Self-assurance and self-determination created self-respect and self-command, bred an innate code of obligations, and inspired both family sense and loyalty, as well as a feeling of social responsibility. There was harmony.

The glamorous plantation legend had its roots in the earlier romanticism of the beginning decades of the nineteenth century, the period of the historical romance of western Europe, of which the plantation literature of the thirties and forties formed the American counterpart. In that period the distinctive traits were already set. The stereotype was taken over by the northern anti-slavery literature for the purpose of emphasizing the contrast between the luxurious life of the whites and the tragic plight of the defenceless, pitiful slaves. This forced the anti-abolitionist apologists to exaggerate more and more the attractive features, particularly as far as race relations were concerned. They even developed a social philosophy which, in the writings of President Thomas R. Dew, Chancellor William Harper, John C. Calhoun, and others, not only rationalized the social stratification, but also (in George Fitzhugh's *Sociology for the South*), while contrasting the evils of modern industrialism with the paternalistic care and providence of the slavery system, idealized the caste system as the model social organization for the world. That also was the standard theme of the *belles lettres* of that period and of the endless discussions about the possible industrialization of the South.

After the war, when the resentful South retired to the refuge of memory, the glory that was the South was heroically exalted. The climax was reached and the legend was definitively fixated when a decade later the North, forgetting the anti-slavery issue, adopted this southern tradition and carried it on in literature, in minstrelsy, on the stage, in popular songs, in pictures, and even in the commercial vulgarization of posters and advertisements, an infallible indication of its strong emotional appeal.

Francis Gaines explains this development by the fact that the plantation legend strongly appeals to "the innate American love of feudalism." He writes: "It is curiously true that however violent may be our profession of political equality, however we may vaunt our democracy, our imaginative interests are keenly appreciative of social gradations, and our romantic hunger is satisfied by some allegory of aristocracy." However, Gaines's interpretation only indicates the psychological disposition, but offers no real explanation for the acceptance of the legend by the North, which thereby repudiated its own anti-slavery tradition.

RECONSTRUCTION AND THE LEGEND

The formation and fixation of the legend can be partially understood as one considers what happened in the political and economic background. After the war, there was general confusion. For three years, the emancipated Negro occupied a nondescript relation to southern society, while local government remained under the control of those who had waged stubborn warfare in support of slavery. The South was still rebellious, resentful; it was struggling by means of the Black Codes to re-establish the old conditions in a new form, finding support in President Andrew Johnson's attitude. Then Congress took things into its own hands, but the South could not believe that the old order was to be overthrown and was startled by the Negro's enfranchisement. The Presidential election of 1872 proved that the new regime was a fact. Before that (particularly after the Presidential and Congressional elections of 1868) not only self-seeking carpet-baggers and scalawags, but also several prominent Southerners, mostly those who had been opposed to secession but had loyally joined the Confederate Army, had accepted the outcome of the war as a *fait accompli*. Trying to make the best of it, they had participated in the new governments and in the drawing up of the new state constitutions. Federal interference had encouraged that movement, and after the election of 1872, several more southern leaders joined the Republican party, realizing that by means of the vote of their former slaves they could maintain their hegemony. Then suddenly the depression of 1873 sobered the North from the intoxication of the liberalism of 1868 and gave rise to the reform movement. The issues of the southern opposition to corruption and "spending" were identical with those of the reform movement of the North. The North had tired of intervention and controversy. The Union was restored. So the outcome of the election of 1874 gave new hope and new strength to the rebellious South, which "had nothing to regret but the dead and the failure." The newly converted southern Republicans repented and deserted the ranks in order to escape social ostracism; others who had not yet openly adopted the creed but silently had voted Republican recognized the turn of the tide. A tremendous reaction followed. The pressure of the "poor whites" and the resentment of the majority, which could not adjust itself to the new order of things and had only temporarily been restrained, became overwhelming.

As a price for the peaceful inauguration of President Hayes (1877) the Republican North turned over the South to the Democrats; the federal troops were withdrawn; and the reconstruction governments, left without northern support, collapsed, being easily, but not without violence, overthrown by their opponents. The Negro was virtually disfranchised; the southern states were "redeemed." The Solid South was a *fait accompli*. The North acquiesced, for it no longer needed the South; the Republican party was safely entrenched and no longer required the Negro vote; the power in the nation had passed from the agriculturist to the industrialist and the financier.

The same change of attitude is found in the general trend of thought as reflected in the historiography concerning the ante-bellum South, the Civil War, and reconstruction. History always has to be rewritten as soon as conditions change. Germany, after the World War, had to rewrite its historical textbooks and now is again reinterpreting history. The fact is that, apart from deliberate propaganda and conscious distortion of the truth for the purpose of proving an *a priori* thesis, the historian is influenced in his assumptions, in his interests, and in the selection of his material by the ideology and the general trend of thought of the period in which he writes. National history strongly believes in the *fait accompli*. If a revolution is successful, its promoters are heroes, their opponents tyrants; if a revolution is unsuccessful, the promoters are dishonest agitators or at least impractical but dangerous idealists. Since the revolution that undid reconstruction, no new revolution in the South has occurred; therefore no need has been felt for a new evaluation. The slogans of the struggle of the southern Democrats—"Negro domination," "carpet-bagger governments," "corruption, frauds, and maladministration because of Negro participation in politics," and so on—have now become "historical verities." As a matter of fact, there had never been a Negro majority in the reconstruction governments, whereas Southerners of standing had prominently participated in them. As for political corruption and "spending," these had not been much worse than in the North, especially in New York, during the same period. However, not facts but opinions about facts determine national history.

The southern plantation legend is the Southerner's version of the past. It was accepted by the North because the charges of "treason" and other utterances of sectional animosity had gradually lost their actuality. The whole attitude of the North towards the South was changed, softened. The desire to forget the regrettable misunderstanding between the states for the sake of the unity of the nation made it necessary to adopt the southern version of the history, at least in part. The *fait accompli* of the undoing of reconstruction stamped reconstruction as a failure and established the southern evaluation of reconstruction governments as historical truth.

National history by its nature is the justification and rationalization of prevailing present-day attitudes. National history is a screen, but the shadows we see moving on it are not the shadows of the past, but our own shadows.

The centres where the tradition was most dearly cherished in reminiscent longing for the good old days were the towns of the South. In the ante-bellum era these had been subsidiary to the country, serving merely as shipping points and as clearing houses for the money crops. They had been, in sentiment and interest, virtually a part of the plantation community. The merchants were plantation factors; the lawyers and doctors had country patrons; many prospering townsmen looked towards plantation retirement as the crown of their careers. In fact before the war the plantation ideal was dominant in southern life. Its laws and usages were as prevalent socially as its economic influence was dominant politically. It set the standards for what was good and desirable. Negroes, "poor whites," and middle classes—all saw in the planter class the embodiment of what they themselves wished to be.

But after the war the towns, representative of the money-dealer, the merchant, and the lawyer, began to acquire a predominant significance in southern life. With the general lack of money, indispensable for a new start, the time merchant was exalted to the first place in the community. At the same time the lawyer came into prominence by reason of his role as legislator and his knowledge of how to make of no effect the thirteenth, fourteenth, and fifteenth amendments to the Constitution. Moreover, the lawyer had to prove over and over again —and people never got tired of hearing it—the justice of the lost cause of the Confederacy and the constitutionality of its action. And, finally, he was indispensable in drawing up contracts for the tenants and in indicating the subterfuges by which to enforce them. The store became the centre of the social and economic life. It was the place where one could hang out on cold and rainy days, meet the people of the local community, transact business, hear the news, and talk politics. With the renting of the land to tenants—instead of using hired Negro labour, which system had been abandoned after some unsuccessful attempts—merchandizing became more lucrative than land-owning. The merchant got either high interest or the land and the animals. This made it practicable for him to operate farms of his own. Aside from sales of land for unpaid taxes, he also could easily buy land at a low price from those who left the section in disgust or despair over the new conditions, wishing to begin a new life outside of the South. In this way, the merchant and the lawyer (followed by the banker and the industrialist) became the new ruling class in the South. The old planter "aristocracy" had to ally itself with this class in order to retain the semblance of its former hegemony. When, during the agricultural depression in the last decades of the nineteenth century, the agrarian movement aroused the farmers against "the hirelings of Wall Street," it seemed for a while as though the political predominance of the merchant (which meant chiefly the preponderance of his attorney, the *lawyer-politician*) would be challenged. This brought the Negro again to the polls. But, finally, common fear of "political niggerism," election frauds, and common dependence on the merchant brought the whites together again, and restored the "solid South."

However, from now on a plebeian faction remained fairly consistently at the helm of the southern Democratic parties. Thus, posing as the champion of "the people" became a *con-*

ditio sine qua non for election; this emphasized personality and demagoguery in politics instead of vital issues. Apart from being a genuine loyal Southerner, the candidate must be able to behave as "a plain man of the people." The election laws were drastically revised in order more effectively to exclude the Negro from voting; the whole election machinery was placed in the hands of the regular professional group in power. The white primary provided a rampart behind which all disagreements could be fought out free of interference from outsiders. Every white man could vote—if he was willing to vote the Democratic ticket.

The Negro was made the scapegoat for class antagonism and has remained so ever since. Of course class cleavage persisted between the small farmers, tenants, urban lower and middle classes, and factory proletariat on the one hand, and, on the other hand, "the best people," the "respectable" citizens, the intelligentsia, bankers, manufacturers, and professional people, "merchants," and a large part of the middle class. But the Negro could be used to obscure the real social and economic issues and to preserve the dominance of the second group, while "machine-control" did the rest.

THE LEGEND AND ANTE-BELLUM SOCIETY

The importance of the merchant—socially, politically—was a new feature in the South; indebtedness was not. Contrary to the legend, there never had been widespread wealth in the South. Too often it had been the merchants and factors in Charleston and Savannah who reaped more from the plantation system than did the planter. The factor's profit consisted not only of the interest on the capital he furnished and on the old debts he carried, but also of the commissions he charged both on the purchases he made for his customer and on the commodities he sold for him. Besides, the factor subtracted liberally from the proceeds for wharfage, freight, insurance, storage, and drayage. Furthermore, most of the money which financed southern agriculture came at high exchange from Boston, New York, and other northern centres. Too often the planter ground out his life in an endless effort to make annual interest for his factor, and then in the end bequeathed to his heirs a mortgaged estate. The extravagance of plantation life and uneconomic management were other causes for bankruptcy. Moreover, the system of tillage rapidly wore out the soil, causing a continuous migration to new virginal regions westward.

One of the outstanding discrepancies of the legend was the tacit assumption that ante-bellum plantation society had been feudalistically tripartite—the lordly planter, the slaves, and the "poor white trash." It is true that the plantation system with its concentration and specialization of labour—consisting of overseers, foremen, millers, blacksmiths, tanners, engineers, painters, bricklayers, plasterers, carpenters, coopers, shoe-makers, harness-makers, mechanics, weavers, shirt-makers, milliners, seamstresses, hostlers, cooks, nurses, plowhands, hoehands and so on—hindered diversification in southern industry and kept the whole community in a state of commercial dependence upon the North and Europe. There was little industrial complexity. Nevertheless, there were white mechanics, wagoners, tavern-keepers and cross-roads store-keepers, small merchants, preachers, doctors, teachers, horse-traders, slave-breeders and dealers, and so forth. There was a host of attorneys feeding on the feuds and lawsuits over land titles and pre-emption claims in the ante-bellum society.

As a matter of fact, more white labour was employed than has sometimes been realized. After 1850, in cotton mills, tobacco factories, ironworks, and in mines, white labour was preferred because slaves were too expensive. For the same reason planters often engaged white labour for digging ditches, for building levees, indeed for every sort of work which would expose the slaves to the hazards of sickness, injury, or death. In New Orleans in the late fifties, whites had already replaced Negroes extensively as cabmen, draymen, and hotel waiters and chambermaids. In this way some types of work began to be characterized as specifically white. Consequently, before the war, white labourers sometimes resorted to strikes in order to prevent the introduction of slaves into their occupations, and tried to restrict slave labour to agriculture. There was constant agitation to exclude the black mechanics, to forbid the apprenticeship of any slave to learn any trade or art, and to protect white labour. In response to the opposition sentiment, not only Georgia but various other states passed laws for the special purpose of regulating the labour of slaves and of free Negroes, whereby "rich men's Negroes" were prohibited from "hiring out" their own time, emancipated Negroes were ordered to leave the state, and the activities of free Negro residents were prescribed. Laws were enacted forbidding manumission by deed or will and preventing the entrance of free Negroes into many states. These laws (1845–60) indicate that before the Civil War there existed a comparatively strong white labour class which had developed a considerable political influence.

The indiscriminate classification as "poor white trash" of all who did not belong to the "aristocratic" ruling class was but the ideal projection of Calhoun's social philosophy, a concept of the social order which was further popularized by the abolitionist authors of the North in order to demonstrate the evil effect of slavery upon white society.

The truth was that even in the agricultural field there was class differentiation. The non-aristocratic whites were not all isolated, stagnating "mountaineers," or degraded "bob-tails," "dirt-eaters," "sandhillers," and "crackers" who lived in the "piney woods" or on the edge of the plantations. They did not all belong to an unproductive, devitalized white proletariat, growing up amid malaria, hookworm, alcoholism, ignorance, and poverty, and forming the rural counterpart of the occupants of the poorhouses and of the slum population of the urban North.

In the fifteen southern states (including the border states) of 1860, the big plantations of 500 acres and more formed not quite three per cent of all the farms. Those who owned 100 slaves or more numbered only 2291 (out of a total white population of 8,036,700), as compared with 8366 who had 50 to 99 slaves, 35,616 who had 20 to 49 slaves, 61,882 who had 10 to 19 slaves, and 275,679 who had less than 10 slaves.[2] From these figures it is evident that the "aristocratic" class was very small indeed and that, if the possession of 20 slaves and more (including women, children, and disabled persons) is taken as the dividing line for a planter class, these planters with their families still formed only three per cent of the total white population. This upper group includes the numerous small planters who made no pretence to spectacular living, but leaves out the 73 per cent of the "slave-owners" that had less than 10 slaves. All the "slave-owners" (346,048 in 1850; 376,635 in 1860) together with their families formed not fully 25 per cent of the total white population. In 1850 out of 1,541,974 white males over fifteen years of age in the South who gave their occupation, 848,815 (in the cotton states alone 523,401) were planters or farmers. This indicates that fully three-fifths even of the southern farmers had no slaves at all. Consequently, instead of the traditional division of patricians and "poor white trash," we find by closer inspection a great variety of economic

---

[2] For the ten cotton states with a total white population of 4,399,921 these figures are respectively: 2151; 7424; 27,965; 43,494; 173,138.

classes in the old South, a continuous gradation from million-aires to paupers. More particularly we discover the presence of a great middle group of common folks who were neither planters nor "poor whites": the self-respecting plain country-men, the backbone of the ante-bellum society, a great class of sober-living, thrifty, independent, and, as a rule, strongly re-ligious proprietors who cultivated their lands themselves or, if they owned a few slaves, worked the land together with their Negroes. In their crude way of living they preserved many traits of rough pioneer days. Compared with New Englanders they were fully a hundred years behind the times in education and in all kinds of improvements. Most of this class were self-sufficient farmers and grew but little cotton; others occupied themselves with cattle raising; others with the turpentine in-dustry. In the Mississippi delta this class was to be found largely as overseers, as patrolmen, or as wood-cutters who sup-plied the steamboats with fuel. But, in the mountains, in some parts of the pine barrens, and on the borders north and west they comprised nearly the entire population. Everywhere else they dwelt as neighbours of the planters and of well-to-do townsmen.

Neither were the social stratification and the social distance, especially in the upland South, so rigid as the legend would make us believe. Just as big planters might go down in bank-ruptcy, so there was a rise from prosperous farmer to small planter and from small planter to big plantation owner. How-ever, such a rise grew more and more difficult as, between 1850 and 1860, the tendency to concentration of wealth increased. The rice plantations in South Carolina were old, but the Cotton Kingdom was of relatively recent origin. All the great cotton lands were first opened by industrious settlers with small means and much energy. Consequently, the relationships between these agricultural classes could not be compared with those of nobility and peasantry in Europe. As a matter of fact, there was relatively little class consciousness. The exclusiveness of Virginia and Charleston was by no means the general rule in the South. The political leadership of the big plantation owners was essentially not different from that of the captains of industry in the North: it was based on their economic position. Moreover, many of the most prominent leaders the South has produced were not of "aristocratic" origin, but rose from the lower social classes (Patrick Henry, Andrew Jackson, John C. Calhoun, Andrew Johnson, Jefferson Davis, and others). No wonder that these different classes could co-operate so thoroughly during the Civil War and that this solidarity remained after it!

SOCIAL CHANGES AFTER THE WAR

After the war the social and economic structure underwent great changes. There was general poverty and almost famine. So there was not only great necessity but also great opportunity for work. However, everybody—planter and small farmer— needed capital. The merchant was willing to provide it but, wishing to safeguard his returns, he urged people to raise money crops. The cotton price was highly attractive. As a result there was a great increase in cotton production. People who had not been planting cotton formerly were forced to raise it. They could do this since fertilizers were coming into general use, making cotton culture possible also on the poorer land. The effect was a breakdown of the ante-bellum self-sufficient farming. People had to buy supplies they formerly produced themselves. Improvement of the roads and the extension of railways encouraged this development still more since cotton could be profitably planted where formerly shipment difficulties had been too great. The financial collapse of the big plantations broke *their* economic self-sufficiency: they had to be divided into smaller tracts. While before the war factors were located chiefly in the big cities, furnishing capital to the big planters, the new feature after the war was the local merchant who supplied everybody with money or its equivalent in seed, fertilizer, and "pantry supplies." The growth of the towns, the extension of cotton culture, and the increase in the number of white cotton-farmers (including the tenants) were the aftermath of the war. The mobility in social ranks gave more people opportunities to rise, since the economic predominance of the "aristocratic" class was broken; on the other hand, many farmers lost their former independence. Their more ambitious children sought escape from the farm to the professions and the greater possibilities of industrial and urban life.

Therefore, it was not the position of the planters alone which was affected. The cotton-raising white farmers and tenants were now all brought into direct competition with the Negro as the white mechanics had been before the war. Emancipation seemed to put both farmers and mechanics in one class with the Negroes. Moreover, the freedmen were forced by economic necessity to try to invade occupations which had been reserved for the lower-class whites. That was exactly the reason why the latter had been opposed to emancipation and its consequence: equality. Even before the war northern abolitionists had had to be careful in the presence of "poor whites" lest they be molested by a mob; the lower-class whites hated the Negro and slavery, but feared emancipation more. In order to save their status, these whites (not yet class conscious and articulate and, until the agrarian movement of the eighties and nineties, not yet politically organized) now clung frantically to the resentful planters, lest they be degraded by the elevation of the blacks. The slogan of "white supremacy" had especial appeal for the lower-class whites, whereas for the "quality folks" it needed not to be claimed but could be taken for granted. The competition into which they were thrown and their pent-up grudge against the Negro embittered the poorer whites. So the struggle began to keep the Negro down.

It was the same ill feeling against the Negro that had been felt by white labourers in the North, periodically between 1830 and 1870, when competition for the same jobs also had resulted in strikes, racial antagonism, riots, and aversion for the abolition crusade of "sentimental philistines and liberty-intoxicated ladies." In 1853 the famous ex-slave Frederick Douglass wrote: "Every hour sees the black man [in the North] elbowed out of employment by some newly arrived immigrant whose hunger and whose color are thought to give him a better title to the place; and so we believe it will continue to be until the last prop is levelled beneath us—white men are becoming house servants, cooks, and stewards on vessels; at hotels, they are becoming porters . . . and barbers—a few years ago and a white barber would have been a curiosity. Now their poles stand on every street. . . ."

The conflict in the South coincided not only with energetic attempts at extermination of the Indians but also with the struggle of white labour in California for the expulsion of the Chinese. The economic conditions of the war-stricken South were not better than those on the Pacific Coast following the industrial and financial crisis. As the Indian had to retreat before the pioneer, so both Negro and Chinese had to leave the field entirely to the white labourer, who wished to free his occupation and his status from the stigma of slavery or coolie-ism. As soon as white labour had made inroads, the "line" was drawn excluding Negro and Chinese from many of their former activities. Both Negro and Chinese retired from the competitive jobs to menial work and less desirable occupations. The rise of craft unionism with its apprentice system helped to consolidate the white artisan's position. Industrial changes and the introduction of machinery made obsolete much of the Negro's skill and training. In agricultural pursuits, however, the competition between the Negro and the white man went on, and in the rural districts racial feeling remained the strongest.

SOUTHERN COMPLEXES: THE LEGEND AND FEAR

In the *mores* of the Pacific Coast the vehement economic struggle left a trauma; in the *mores* of the South the Civil War left two complexes. The first were the associations connected with the plantation legend; the second was fear.

The legend determined the Negro's place and set the standard for interracial relationships. This complex, charged with the resentment of the reconstruction period, is still extremely sensitive. Disfranchisement of the Negro and his exclusion from jury service and the primaries; segregation of schools, churches, hospitals, and cemeteries; Jim Crow laws; taboos on intermarriage, on eating and shaking hands with coloured people, on tipping the hat to a coloured woman, on addressing Negroes as Mr., Mrs., or Miss have been inspired by it. All these legal measures and conventions came from the desire for the restoration of racial relations according to the standard of the tradition, the restitution of the white man and the Negro to their respective "places." The issue of white prestige has also affected the administration of justice: there is a tendency to punish minor offences disproportionately in order to remind the Negro of his place or to administer a lesson of deterrence. For the same reason, a coloured man cannot always easily find justice in the courts in cases in which a white man is involved. In some regions the white man who kills a Negro is easily excused, while the Negro who kills a white man, even in defence of himself or his wife, may be lynched. In the plantation districts the owner or the manager often administers justice himself; the whipping of an unwilling Negro is not everywhere an exception. "The Negro has no rights that white men must respect."

Because of the legend no objective attitude towards the reconstruction period is possible. "The agony following the surrender of Lee" has been so great that people simply cannot see anything but the failures of Negro participation in politics. In the fourth chapter were mentioned the objections to Irish, Jewish, and Italian influence in politics. There were anti-Irish riots near Boston as early as 1834, and ten years later several Irish Catholic churches were burned in Philadelphia; but these outrages belong to the past. The southern feeling against large-scale Negro suffrage, however, is still aggressive; the concept of the reconstruction period has too many painful associations.

In a "progressive" southern state in which during reconstruction days the fight with the carpet-baggers was particularly virulent, I happened to visit a place where a referendum was being held on the question of adopting a city-manager charter. Negro voters had been aroused by a (northern) city employee who led them to the polls. Immediately the old resentment of the time when the Negro vote wielded the balance of power was stirred to life again: the revival of the plebeian "Red Shirts" of the agrarian revolt was passionately discussed. A white Negro-sympathizer explained to me that it had been ill-advised of the Negroes to participate in this vote, especially since the majority of them had lent themselves as instruments of the corrupt city administration; ill feeling against the Negro was aroused by this action, which would make it very difficult to do anything for him in the near future. . . . At the next referendum, a coloured preacher withheld the Negroes from voting.

Indeed, the passions of the reconstruction period have impressed themselves ineffaceably on the minds of the white people. One can often hear educated white men who heartily sympathize with the Negro, exert themselves for his advancement, and are strongly opposed to modern Ku-Klux Klan movements, speak with grateful respect of the original Ku-Klux Klan—"which intended regulation, not punishment, and restored the feeling of security"—and recall the humiliation they felt in their youth when they had to collect the mail from the hands of illiterate Negro postmasters. Such people, looking back upon the process of undoing reconstruction—with its violence, intimidation, open bribery, stuffing ballot boxes, manipulation or falsification of election returns, use of tissue ballots, etc., all serving to eliminate Negro voters—will not defend those practices. Nevertheless, they cannot forget the impressions of their early youth, which have left a feeling of satisfaction and liberation, and the sincere conviction that the result has also been to the benefit of the Negro. The history of the Democratic "Red Shirts" in South Carolina reminds one strongly of the rise of the Nazis in Germany; the parallels are striking. One liberal Southerner, whose work is in the field of Negro education, was visibly shocked when I told him of a white politician in the North who, before his election, had given a breakfast in honour of several Negro leaders, a breakfast which I had attended. It was not the idea of eating together which confounded him so much, but the act of soliciting Negro votes on the part of the white man; it at once evoked the associations connected with the "carpet-bagger regime" and "white supremacy." Negro support or "fraternizing with Negroes" is still a damning charge against a candidate in the South.

If this is still the attitude of educated white people, one can easily imagine what the reactions of Southerners must have been in 1865 and later. There was the usual after-war demoralization; there was a general social disorganization with crime and violence; there was extreme poverty; there were despised northern speculators and rapacious federal cotton agents; there was the "freebooting carnival" of carpet-baggers and scala-wags; there were feelings of defeat and bitterness over lost homes and properties; there was the emancipation of the slaves, "stolen property" that had been driven away like the horses, mules, and cattle. There still were coloured soldiers marching around, the enemies of yesterday since they had been enlisted by the Union government during the war. There were the freedmen, a constant source of irritation, noisily and "impudently" rejoicing in the feeling of new freedom; there was the general vagrancy; there was the spirit of revenge. There were the old slaves, who during the war and since had remained on the plantation; there were the other slaves who loyally and valiantly had stood by their masters on the battle-field; there was the ante-bellum pattern.

How could the South—for years and years educated in the faith of caste and inequality, steeped in the theology which justified slavery by Scriptural evidence, and accustomed to con-sider the Negro as a chattel, as a labour commodity—suddenly treat him as a person and recognize him, emancipated against his will, as a fellow-citizen and a voter? Social equality was in-conceivable. People simply could not believe that the Negro would make a reliable free labourer, and the conduct of many freedmen seemed to justify such pessimism. The Black Codes —passed, shortly after Lincoln's death and Johnson's accession, to meet the immediate necessities of the labour situation and to provide for continued subordination—reflected the public opinion. This was a white man's government, and "in the sight of God and the light of reason" a Negro suffrage was impos-sible. What else could have been expected but an attitude of self-defence, especially since Negro suffrage combined with the disfranchisement of the former "rebels" meant the curbing of the political power of the southern whites, the possibility of confiscation and redistribution of land, the protection of the interests of northern industry and capital, and the safeguarding of the predominance of the Republican party in the country? The claim to superiority and the right to rule on the part of the Southerners was not simply injustice or mere wickedness; it was illusion. It was their rationalization of a situation, exactly as "manifest destiny" rationalized the economic desire for expansion.

Although there were temporary military occupation, Freedmen's Bureau activities, incidental intervention of federal bayonets in the elections of the South, and occasional repression or practice of violence, the North refrained from systematically and effectively imposing its will. Its main interest was the restoration of the Union and the frustration of the power of the southern oligarchy; but it was never thoroughly convinced of the equality of the Negro. Later, the desire for reconciliation and the demands of domestic politics prevented the North and the Republican party from protesting when, in most of the southern states, the great mass of the Negro population was disfranchised. The people of the entire country were more or less reconciled to allowing the South to deal with the Negro problem in its own way.

THE BLACK SPECTRE RULES THE SOUTH

Meanwhile, although the Negro is for all practical purposes out of southern politics, although Republicanism except in the border states is a lost cause, although the supremacy of the white race is fully established and the right of the white people to govern has been admitted by the North, the South still has not been able to free itself from the thrall of the Negro spectre. Reconstruction drove the white people to unite solidly against their "oppressors"; the factional fights caused by the agrarian movement resulted in re-establishing that unity. From then until now the political solidarity of the South has been an established fact. The white men of that section have stood together in political matters, often sacrificing their individual convictions upon questions of national politics. Consequently, there has been practically but one political party in the South, and that a white man's party; and there has been but one vital issue, namely, the maintenance of white supremacy. Agitation may subside for a number of years, but the old issue is always in the background: southern politics move in the shadow of the past. Not only southern *politics!* If one looks through the files of the periodicals of the last thirty-five years or through the bibliographies, the amount of essentially apologetic literature produced by Southerners is simply astonishing—if not pathetic. The same attitude can be observed in the history classes of southern universities. The Civil War and reconstruction issues, and everything connected with them, have grown into a monomania. From time to time liberal spirits earnestly try to free themselves and their section from the obsession and struggle bravely against traditionalism and conformity, but their voices are shouted down. Sometimes, when one thinks that liberation is approaching, a single incident stirs the emotions. Again there is resort to the old pattern. No infringement of the tradition escapes the attention of the Daughters of the Confederacy and other guardians of the past and of public opinion. This monomania has been the obstacle met by progressive minds hoping to change the general attitude—from Generals Lee and Longstreet on up to the present.

The South is absorbed in itself; specifically, the South is absorbed in the Negro. In politics there is still the doctrine that a division of the white voters of the South into two parties would pave the way for "the return of the Negro to power," and that, therefore, the continued political solidarity is necessary to prevent the Republican party from "forcing Negro rule upon the people of the South." "Division of the white votes, combined with Negro suffrage [so it is argued], would inevitably produce corruption, buying the Negro by social privileges. Dividing politically would mean destroying the defences of the social integrity of the white society. Political equality would lead to social equality; and the two together would be the stepping stone to miscegenation."

On the other hand, the South has lost its national political importance. Its one-party system implies voting for anything bearing the Democratic label; so there is little doubt before a national election as to the direction of the southern vote. This means that the the South is politically unprincipled and therefore sterile, that it is a negligible political factor. National elections in the South involve no contest, are nothing more than a perfunctory compliance with the forms of the Constitution, and have no significance to the South or to the nation at large. For this reason no sufficient consideration can be given to the great economic and political questions which divide the people of the rest of the nation and concern the South's own progress and welfare. Although there is undoubtedly an increase in Republican votes at the Presidential elections in the industrialized southern states, the break in the solid southern front in 1928 is no indication that public opinion really is changing. It means only that the Roman Catholicism and "wetness" of Alfred E. Smith clashed with another symptom of southern solidarity, i.e., the (dry) "southern Christianity," of which we shall speak later on. On the contrary the "lily-white" Republican movement in the South, which did not shrink even from denying the past and allying itself with the Ku-Klux Klan and with racial and religious fanatics in order to regain a foothold, proves how strong the feelings still are. As a matter of fact during the 1928 election racial sentiment was appealed to more than it had been in many years. Moreover, there are indications of the existence of understandings between local Republican nuclei and the Democratic machine, sometimes based on personal connexions and sometimes on exchange of patronage, understandings which also sometimes make Republican campaigns mere sham battles frustrating effective opposition within the Democratic ranks.

However, the racial issue is not only an obsession. It also represents political capital which can be successfully exploited for political campaigns: Negro-bating is still very common. A politician cannot afford to go against the deep-seated sentiments of his constituents and hope to be elected. Apart from this, it is also in the interests of placemen and spoilsmen to maintain the force of patronage-animated party fealty.

As the South concentrated itself on itself, its past, and its civilization, it arrested development and wasted the energy necessary for building up its resources and preparing for the future. The disorganization after the Civil War imprinted on its mind the dread of anything that might disintegrate its unity. The South looks backward, not forward. Hence, despite the boisterous ballyhoo of the boosters of a "New South," despite some industrialization, the prevailing tendency of the South is still fear of change and "progress." It describes its stolidity as "dread of the accelerating speed of modern life with its incessant, infinite extension of energy and effort without a specific goal, its perpetual disadjustment, its lack of stability; industrialism with its inevitable influx of Northerners, its labor problems and other disintegrating influences; materialism with its inherent dispensation of all leveling collectivism, its standardized commonplaceness, its spiritual poverty, and its dehumanization of life which threaten to endanger the characteristic cultural values of the South."

RELIGION AS A SOUTHERN SOLACE

The more that innovations were introduced, the more the South turned away from liberalism and the concept of evolution. Self-preservation remained the dominating trait. There is still the tendency, however absent in practice, to stress and exalt by lip service democracy as it has been revealed to the South —the "grand old rock-ribbed Democracy." Another rallying point is "southern Christianity"—"the faith once for all delivered to the saints." Was it not "that old-time religion" that through circuit-rider and revivalist had been the organizing force of pioneer social life in the early South? When the frontier faith had become domesticated into the rural church, had not the churches and camp meetings been the sole recreation and consolation, aside from barbecues and court days, for the numerous class of common folks? What was more natural than that, in the convulsive years after the war, and later during the agricultural depression, people should flee anew from the toil and turmoil of every day into the soothing refuge of "that old-time religion," the only form of organization they knew? What more natural than that, in the tension of self-isolation and monomania, these fundamentalist farmers who had now come to power should cling to it and jealously guard it? Meanwhile, feverish emotionalism passed into religious conservatism and theological simplicity.

Under these circumstances religion could not but penetrate the domain of southern political life, resulting sometimes in a denominational control of public and intellectual life, sometimes in participation in the general mood of intolerance and attempts at suppression of freedom of speech and thought, and sometimes in a stubborn resistance to, if not frustration of, all creative effort. In the consciousness of the South, solidarity in matters of religion is as well established as solidarity in politics.

It is not only that religion contributes to political and social life; the dominating social pattern also influences religious life. The reunion of the Methodist Church South with the northern Methodist Episcopal Church has been blocked for many years by the recollections of the Civil War and reconstruction, and by the fear that the Negroes of the northern church might in some way be forced upon the southern church. The Negro issue was as vital as it had been in 1844, when they separated, to be followed by the Baptists in 1845.

Since pastors and preachers defended "the providential trust of the southern people" during slavery times, it is not surprising that their modern successors should be champions of the existing social order. It is the custom of men to make divine approval bear the burden of that to which they have become habituated and of that which they desire. However, it was not necessary to invoke such approval for the schism between the white and the coloured churches. Race discrimination was so respectable an attitude that the colour line could be drawn in all frankness without theological rationalization or subterfuge of any sort. If, therefore, a sign outside a church in a southern city reads: "We offer riches to the poor, friendliness to the friendless, comfort to the sorrowing—a welcome to all, step in," every Negro child in that section of the country knows that the invitation is meant for him as little as the "free barbecue for all" advertised as an attractive feature of a public sale. That was also learned by a Negro intellectual who, entering a Y.M.C.A. (on the cornerstone of which was written "for the love of Christ") merely to get some information, was informed even before he could frame his question, "Negroes are not allowed in here." It was not until the second decade of the twentieth century that Protestant church organizations made any effort to break down the restrictions placed upon mere colour.

Wherever we look, we find the symptoms and expressions of that extreme craving for self-preservation which causes a social strain and a tension in the southern spiritual and intellectual atmosphere, even stronger than the pressure towards uniformity born of self-defence we found in the North.[3]

In one of the cities of the South I saw a beautiful big old tree right in the middle of a street. Although it blocks modern traffic—many accidents occur because of it—it cannot be removed because its task is perpetually and eternally to remind the Negroes of the hanging of some coloured rebels from its branches many many years ago. It is an ever-warning monument to white supremacy. That tree seems to me to be a symbol of what the Negro problem and the obsession about white prestige are to the South: it roots in the past, it cannot be removed, and it blocks the way.

Dispassionate discussion of the *mores* is impossible, for prejudice does not allow analysis but seeks justification and rationalization. As regards the attitude towards the Negro, there has been plenty of rationalization: the testimony of the Bible has been and still is invoked as evidence, anthropological measurements of the skull have been adduced, the brain weight has been cited, psychological theories have been resorted to, mental tests have been applied, criminal statistics have been quoted. However, the final judgment of unbiased science puts a question mark. Nevertheless, the deeply rooted conviction that the Negro is an inferior creation remains intact. And in the midst of an increasing mixed race of the South's own begetting we hear, as we hear in the North and in the West, the clamour for purity of race enforced by legal sanction. Virginia, most concerned with the anxiety for racial integrity, has installed a regular genealogical service whose task it is to expel from white society everyone tainted with a drop of dubious blood. Louisi-

[3] See Chapter IV.

ana, wiser, closely guards the secrets of the old marriage registrations of the church. . . .

FEAR

It is not fear of Negro domination alone that keeps the South in thrall. Since the violent slave revolution of Santo Domingo and Haiti (1804) and particularly since the insurrections of Denmark Vesey (1822) and Nat Turner (1831), there has always been a fear of the Negro himself. This fear was increased during the period of lawlessness immediately after the war, when the new freedom had intoxicated the Negroes, thousands had forsaken the rural districts and flocked to the towns, armed Negro soldiers roamed through the country within easy reach of liquor, and both life and property were regarded as unsafe. Although it was not included in the plantation legend, even before the war the Negro had a reputation for criminality. The crime and violence committed under the chaotic conditions of reconstruction days strengthened that opinion. "Rape was the foul daughter of reconstruction." "It was not until the original Ku-Klux Klan began to ride that white women felt some sense of security." These quotations serve to characterize the situation. It is not important how many—well-proved, actual—attempts to rape were made in the general demoralization of those days; it *is* significant that a widespread fear existed which has left a deep impression on the southern mind. Negro and rape form a fixed association. The tradition of chivalry demanded protection of the women and bloody revenge for their insulters. However, apart from actual rape, other circumstances were likely to create an equally great excitement. Many of the young men had died, and in the general poverty after the war it was very difficult for their widows to find a living. The result was that such persons sometimes had relations with Negroes. A chronicler of that time wrote: "In those districts of South Carolina where the black population was densest, and the poor whites by consequence most degraded, these unnatural unions were more frequent than anywhere else. In every case, without exception, it was a woman of the lowest class, generally a 'sandhiller' who, having lost in war her only supporter, 'took up with a likely nigger' to save her children from absolute famine."

The desperate struggle of the lower-class whites for preservation of their status explains the extreme violence of their reaction in such cases. However, "southern chivalry" alone does not determine present attitudes. There are other traditions. During the period of confusion after the war, the whites in order to restore public security resorted to methods of intimidation of the Negroes for the purpose of reminding them of their place. The Ku-Klux Klan was born, and the Ku-Klux Klan spread. There had been murders and atrocities of blacks against blacks, of whites against whites, of blacks against whites, and of whites against blacks; but the Ku-Klux Klan movement endeavoured to control the conduct of the former slaves and of those whites who favoured the blacks. Whites combined to suppress lawlessness by lawless methods. "Regulation" developed into a wave of riots and crime, a bloodthirsty guerrilla warfare, since the secrecy and covert activities of the Klan made it easy for anybody to use its insignia and costumes in acts of violence. The riders for the planters drove the Negroes back to the plantations; the "poor whites" molested coloured workers or successful Negro farmers. It was a revival of the frontier spirit expressing itself in organized violence—the same spirit found in the California of the gold-rush period. Lynch law is essentially a fruit of frontier conditions with population sparse, officials few, amateurish, and easy-going, and legal machinery consequently inadequate. That it prevailed in the ante-bellum South to a degree comparable at all to that in the mining camps was doubtless due to the thinness of settlement and to the occasional hysteria over rapes and rumours of revolts by Negroes.

The practice of "regulation" and the institution of "regulators," committees of vigilance, and even bands of disguised men were not new phenomena of the post-war era. Such methods had been employed by the most responsible and substantial citizens, labouring to maintain social order in the face of the law's desuetude. A mere step further in that direction lay outright lynch law. The facts refute the oft-asserted southern tradition that Negroes never violated white women before slavery was abolished, whereas many of the lynchings described are identical with what nowadays still actually happens (breaking into jail, burning alive at the stake, mock trial, man-hunt with bloodhounds, etc.). Suspicion of rape or accusation of robbery or of murder was a sufficient reason for lynching then as now, while attempts to make an attack on master, mistress, or overseer were likely to grow into a rumour of an insurrection as the reports flew over the countryside, and to cause panic and outbursts of violence.[4] The powerful influence these rumours of conspiracy and revolt had on public opinion and policy survives in the public fright and fervour of our times—even in a "modern" city such as Atlanta—when rumours of communistic agitation among Negroes alarm the white population, the Negro intellectuals now being suspected of preaching incendiary notions like the free persons of colour in the past.

It is not true that lynchings and the Ku-Klux Klan are products of reconstruction, and that reconstruction should be

[4] During slavery two influences restricted lynchings. First, slaves were property to the loss of which the slave-owner strongly objected. Second, the attraction of the man-hunt which plays such a dominating part in modern lynching was then provided for by the hunt for runaway slaves, in which the "poor whites" eagerly participated.

held responsible for these phenomena when they occur nowadays. Even outside of the South we find these extra-legal organizations, "vigilantes," who terrorize striking workingmen in California and elsewhere, with the tolerance if not the connivance of the police. At the bottom of this disrespect for the law are some specific American characteristics: the intense individualism which causes permanent fears of executive despotism, expressed in the Jeffersonian doctrine that "that government is best which governs least." For the same reason American people as a rule still prefer to think of government in terms of what they as persons can get out of it and only hesitatingly accept the principle of the administration of government by experts. As long as the citizen does not directly lose money as a result of the inefficiency of office-holders, he does not care. Hence the lack of that accepted police control which is especially characteristic of continental Europe. In the South, with its tradition of homicides, this tendency is accentuated. But if one asks for an explanation, the complex of the reconstruction era is so dominating that, by way of projection, the North and the Negro at once are blamed for it. Reconstruction has absorbed all disagreeable experiences and is responsible for all attitudes. However, it is true that, whereas before the war lynchings and Klan formations were incidental and local, during reconstruction they became more general and organized.

In that period the Ku-Klux Klan and similar organizations served also to intimidate Negro voters and to terrorize elections. Later on, fear for the decline of white prestige, rumours of Negro insubordination, competition, any change in the existing order, etc., made people resort again to these attitudes, which had become part of the *mores.* In the days of depression, when competition for the same jobs is strongest, and in times of general excitement or emotional tension, rumour of rape, the hysterical story of a girl, a white man insulted by a Negro, a boasting Negro, may cause lynchings. Part of the persistence of this attitude doubtless is due to isolation, lack of escape from the dullness and drudgery of the poverty-stricken everyday life, desire for social importance, lack of wholesome recreation, suppressed wishes, the low spiritual and intellectual level, the strain of the southern monomania, and the social disintegration of the shifting tenant and cropper class.

Southern society has not yet developed effective means to check this evil because it still regards the Negro as subhuman. Furthermore, the concept of white supremacy blocks here—in contrast with the proud tradition of Anglo-Saxon colonial administration—the way to equality of justice because of the traditional spirit of disrespect for the law and for human life. Often rural peace officers fail to resist the mob effectively, being either in connivance with it, or indifferent, or unwilling to risk their lives protecting a "nigger," or not daring to go against the desires of the local electorate upon which they depend for their jobs. The presence at lynchings of the "best people" in the community; justification by leading politicians, judges, preachers, and businessmen; violent reactions to criticism; silent acquiescence on the part of leading citizens; the virtual immunity of the depraved lynchers from apprehension, indictment, and conviction; and the apathy of the general public show that this lawlessness is still part of the *mores*.

This does not mean that there is not a growing group of educated Southerners who thoroughly condemn and feel ashamed of these outrages. But their voices, as far as they are heard in public, have not yet been able to change the spirit. It is not only lynching, mobbing, and "Kluxery"; it is the way in which Negroes are convicted, punished, and as convicts in the prisons and camps are treated and leased to contractors; it is use that is made of the vagrancy laws; it is the attitude of juries and courts; it is recurrent police brutality. Lynchings, tar-and-feather parties, and other forms of coercive mob behaviour are only different ways in which the spirit of social irresponsibility expresses itself. Of course, there are high-minded individuals who do not discriminate between white criminals and coloured, individuals also who display the paternalistic attitude of the plantation legend; but it is not the petty officer alone whose action reflects the prevailing opinion about the Negro. That same spirit is found in the complacency and leniency with which juries and courts deal with the slaying of one Negro by another unless robbery or some other dishonourable motive is involved, or in the matter-of-course way in which the planter, governed by atavistic instincts of ownership, traditions of a "feudal" code of honour, aversion to police interference, and direct economic motives, takes the law into his own hands as far as "his" Negroes are concerned, and even protects and defends them against the forces of law and order.

The Commission on Interracial Co-operation, backed up by church conferences, women's associations, and the like, has been active in educating popular opinion through publicity, schools, and colleges. The considerable decrease in the number of lynchings is attributed to its influence. Courses in interracial problems are offered at universities; in summer schools and special conferences attention is given to the Negro problem; local committees study race relationships and try to develop mutual understanding and higher standards of public morality; the youth in high school hears more about Negro achievements than formerly; there is improvement in the attitude of the press; but—there is still a long way to go before the spirit of "the Negro has no rights that white men must respect" will be regenerated.

THE NEGRO: AMERICAN YET ALIEN

Many people, pointing to the contrast between the Negroes in Africa and the educated Negroes in the United States, claim that, despite all the humiliations and sufferings, slavery has been to the benefit of the coloured people. Others doubt whether for the majority of the Negroes the present situation is any better than their plight during slavery.

As was stated above, during slavery there was the ingrained feeling among the whites that the Negro slaves were chattels, their property by natural right, existing for the special purpose of raising cotton, sugar, and rice. The better type of slave-owners took good care of their slaves not only out of humanitarian feelings but also because of the considerable value they represented. The slaves were considered a kind of animal to whom one could be attached as one is attached to a faithful dog or to a favourite riding horse. Generations of American nativity made no difference nor did the fact that the Negro accepted the dress, language, religion, and other fundamentals of white civilization. The Negro remained an alien.

The Negro is still regarded as an alien. White Americans are as a rule disagreeably surprised if their question, "What do you think of the Negro?" is answered by, "I think the Negro is so thoroughly American." The comparison of the faithful dog is still *en vogue*. Nothing humiliating is meant by it; on the contrary, it is often interpreted in such a way as to mean a strong mutual attachment. I am even inclined to think that it often is just a human feeling based on many years of intercourse and common experience and that all this high-sounding talk is nothing but rationalization, an excuse to reconcile personal feelings with current notions. White men hostile to the Negro in general will protect and help the individual Negro of their acquaintance whom they completely detach in their thinking from all other Negroes. Nevertheless, the Negro remains an alien.

Emancipation had found the Negroes unprepared for the new responsibilities. The situation was quite different from what happened in the rural districts after the Russian revolution, when the returned peasant soldiers began to divide the great landholdings before the revolutionary government of the industrial proletariat of the cities was safely established. In the South there had not been a gradually growing resistance, developing in revolutionary organization and climaxing in a revolt. There was not that sentimental attachment of the peasant to the soil which is characteristic of primitive rural economy. As far as there was attachment, it was between the slave and his "white folks." It was the war between the whites that brought emancipation as its inevitable result. But there was for the freedman no stability on which to fall back. There was no community, no organization to which to resort. The freedmen had no homes, no money, no food. Apart from the rations the Union troops provided, stealing was the only means by which they could live. They were helpless. There was no place for them in society.

Some had foreseen this; they remained on the plantations. Booker T. Washington writes in his *Up from Slavery:*

> The wild rejoicing on the part of the emancipated coloured people lasted but for a brief period, for I noticed that by the time they returned to their cabins there was a change in their feelings. The great responsibility of being free, of having charge of themselves, of having to think and plan for themselves and their children, seemed to take possession of them. . . . [There] were the questions of a home, a living, the rearing of children, education, citizenship, and the establishment and support of churches. . . . Gradually, one by one, stealthily at first, the older slaves began to wander from the slave quarters back to the "big house" to have a whispered conversation with their former owners as to the future.

There was no economic basis for the new freedom. Edwin R. Embree makes the same point as a central theme of his review of the Negroes' struggle:

> By the Emancipation Proclamation the Negro was given freedom of person only. He was not given property or tools or any means of making a livelihood . . . and there was no way to provide automatically the other essentials of a free people in a complex society. The freedmen, therefore, slowly and painfully had to win every kind of real independence: education, economic status, responsibility, self-development.

The freedmen had to fall back on the whites for their living, which implied that the old habits regained strength.

Then came the efforts of the whites to re-establish white supremacy, efforts tending to bring the Negroes back to the plantation, to impress upon them their inferior status, their subordination to all the whites; efforts to teach them that it was better, or at least safer, not to participate in politics.

In this way their economic dependency found its expression in their status. After some attempts on the part of the plantation owners to introduce a system of hiring labour—attempts which were frustrated by the scarcity of money, the extreme poverty of the freedmen, and the competition among the employers—the tenant and share-cropper system was adopted which—through replacing slavery by legally sanctioned peonage—guaranteed stable labour [5] to the land-owner and security of livelihood to the Negro.

THE NEGRO'S "PLACE"

So the Negro was forced back to his "place." What that place really is is a little difficult to describe. It means that the Negro

---

[5] The West and the East for a long time safeguarded stability of labour by importing contract labour. The institution of indentured servants in the American colonies served the same purpose.

has to remain at the bottom of the social scale. There is no such thing as "beginning at the bottom and working to the top." However competent, however diligent, the Negro who works for the average white corporation very soon finds himself at the limit of advancement. On the other hand, if a Negro rises, he will be careful not to become conspicuous, lest he be accused of putting on airs and thus arouse resentment. The appearance of his house or his automobile may not be too attractive. "Keeping the Negro in his place" means in the rural districts that no Negro can rise to land-ownership unless he has some white man as a protector who encourages him, advances the money, settles the legal and administrative difficulties, and protects him against aggression. Even then he cannot become a land-owner unless he is "acceptable," i.e., punctiliously servile to the whites and not one to find fault with existing educational, social, political, and economic conditions. "Keeping the Negro in his place" is the mechanism of the white man for preserving his racial and social integrity; at the same time, it obliges him to assume a benevolent attitude and to provide for his dependents. "Keeping the Negro in his place" implies that the Negro tenant or share-cropper may not ask questions about the accuracy of the landlord's account. It means impressing upon the Negro a permanent feeling of inferiority. Experience or example has taught him that competition and jealousy on the part of the lower classes of whites often form an almost unsurpassable obstacle to his progress. "Keeping the Negro in his place" therefore means either a lapsing into a "what is the use" attitude after some vain effort to get ahead, or taking it easy, being improvident and avoiding trouble; it causes an attitude of apathy, fatalism, trust in God, and dependency on the white people. It results in corruption of character and morals, resort to lying, adulation, servility.

"Keeping the Negro in his place" creates a permanent pressure on the wage level of the lower classes of the white group, which, fearing to be supplanted by Negro labour, finds its main reward in suffrage and in public deference from the Negro. It signifies that the Negro must remain poor and drag the white man down with him. It means that depression and economic need urge the whites to take over Negro jobs, leaving the Negroes as a burden on the community. It means the perpetuation of a disorganized, shifting, ignorant, and degenerate pariah group in which crime and disease flourish and which forms a permanent danger to society.

"Keeping the Negro in his place" is an especially disheartening doctrine for the educated Negro because it does not allow for discrimination between the coloured people, and because the practice of daily life differs so entirely from the basic principles of American democracy, the principles of freedom and equality for all, the principle of equality of opportunity as taught in the schools. The difficulties confronted by the educated Negro may be illustrated by a few examples.

The white president of a long-established Negro institution for higher learning gave a reception at which white and coloured citizens interested in Negro education could meet me, the white citizens not being invited but simply given notice. Many of the white citizens present were there for the first time and were obviously embarrassed by finding a mixed group. One of these was the wife of a white educator whose life work is Negro advancement. The Negroes were favourably impressed by her presence at this occasion. The lady, however, hardly recovered from this unusual and unforeseen experience, was visibly discomforted when ice cream was served—which gave an entirely new aspect to this social function. Of course her behaviour did not escape the attention of the highly cultured Negro guests whose unperturbed faces did not betray any emotion.

In an elevator is an educated Negro woman. At the next stop a white man enters the car and automatically takes off his hat. The elevator stops once more, and another white man steps in. Immediately, the first man puts his hat on again lest the other man take exception to his courtesy towards a "negress."

In another southern town a young coloured college girl left a white store hurriedly and quite inadvertently jostled a white man who was passing on the sidewalk. Unhesitatingly, this man knocked the girl down and walked on.

In a dormitory of a coloured university was a practically white Negro girl who was shunned by the male students. She was never taken out on a drive, not so much because the boys had anything against her as because it was too dangerous for them to do so, since policemen might mistake her for a white girl, which would involve grave consequences.

In a white denominational institution a coloured boy was enrolled who—through his mother—was partly Indian and passed as a Latin American. Because of his educational achievements, sportsmanlike qualities, and general character, he was highly esteemed by his fellow-students and played a leading role in student organizations. This lasted for seven years when —one month before his last examination—it was suddenly discovered that he was a Negro. The same day the other students demanded his dismissal, which was granted lest they leave the institution.

A Negro college boy was driving his aunt in their motor car along the highway at night when they passed a wrecked automobile. The two white girls in the car evidently needed help. The boy at once wanted to stop but was prevented by his aunt, who foresaw complications should white men find the boy with the white girls at night; it might lead to a lynching. So they drove on and gave notice of the accident in the next village. Cases like this are by no means exceptional.

A Negro college girl had a serious automobile accident. She was taken to the hospital in the next town but was refused because she was coloured. She had to be transported to a house from which a telephone call was sent to a far-off Negro hospital. By the time the hospital car arrived, the girl was dead.

What shall the educated Negro do? Some emigrated to foreign countries but, land, language, and people being unfamiliar, they became homesick. Longing for America, despite its discriminations, they finally returned. Others migrated to the North but, being essentially southern, found conditions uncongenial and came back. This does not mean that there is not resentment. The strain that social life puts on them is strongly resented, especially the uncertainty as to what "place" implies in all possible situations. "Place" differs in the different parts of the South: what here is accepted is impossible in the adjoining county. Then the notions of individual white people differ greatly. New, unusual situations are particularly difficult. An educated Negro who has been sitting in conference with prominent whites may be insulted by a taxi-driver the next moment. Richard Harrison, who played with distinction the part of "the Lawd" in *The Green Pastures,* on concluding the southern tour in Texas was given a reception by the governor of the state in the governor's mansion and received an ovation from the leading white citizens who had come to meet him and do him honour; that night he was refused a berth on the train and had to make an all-night trip sitting up in the shabby "Jim Crow coach." It is a little-known fact that Richard Harrison died of a cold contracted during an overnight stay in an unheated railway station, as no hotel was willing to give him a room. To meet such situations requires an extraordinary adaptability on the Negro's part.

Negroes grown up in the North and coming to the South find—even under the favourable circumstances of segregation

and the isolation of Negro institutions of higher learning—
the greatest difficulty in accommodating themselves. Not that
discrimination does not exist in the North: in the North they
are also aliens and share in the existing prejudices against
aliens. Their visibility is an added impediment to absorption,
although for the slightly coloured ones "passing" is easier in
the North than it is in the South. This "passing" is not sought
so much because of the desire for social intercourse with the
white group as because of the wish to escape the discriminations
and disabilities.[6] But there is still the danger of being detected.
A coloured woman passed for white in order to obtain a job
in a first-class white store. One day she decided to have a new
hat and wished her husband to help her select it. The husband
being of darker complexion, they went to another store in
order to avoid suspicion. There, however, they were waited on
by a girl who for three years had been working with her in the
first store. As soon as she realized what would happen, she told
her husband to go away. Too late! The girl asked her who the
coloured man was. She denied having anything to do with that
man, whereupon the girl said: "Did you not know that I am
coloured too?"

Another handicap for the Negro in the North as compared
with the immigrant is the partial adoption of the southern
legend which has put on him an ineffaceable stamp. Finally,
there are the reminiscences of the disturbances following the
mass immigration of southern Negroes during and after the
World War. Nevertheless, the Negro enjoys an amount of
freedom in the North unsurpassed by anything he has anywhere in the South. On the other hand, the paternalistic and
often cordial attitude towards the individual Negro, symptomatic of the South, is lacking in the North.

[6] The same holds true for the pathetic efforts to bleach the skin and
straighten the hair in an attempt to lose marks of identification.

It is not surprising that the resentment caused by the manifold discriminations seeks a way out. It cannot be denied that many educated Negroes have a great interest in communism and the Soviet experiment. The Russian form of state socialism appeals to them especially as it would supposedly overcome the difficulties of employment and racial barriers. It is remarkable how many intellectual Negroes have actually spent some time in Russia or at least visited there. Nevertheless, I have been struck by three aspects of these communistic sympathies. In the first place, I found an adolescent kind of parlour communism which is also fairly well represented among white employees in many of the New Deal agencies in Washington. In the second place, I saw Negro communistic agitators at work in a meeting, and noted that in all details (even in their voices) they resembled communistic agitators in other parts of the world. A highly artificial pattern! Although there are sufficient grievances with which soap-box orators can stir up sentiment, this does not mean that the basic communistic doctrines take with the public. In the third place, I found among confessed Negro communists, along with a warm sympathy for the doctrine, a highly critical attitude towards the communistic achievements in Russia, which often revealed a fundamental, but unconscious, "typically American" (i.e., capitalistic) approach. As far as it was possible for me to get an impression of what is going on among coloured workingmen, I understand that communistic sentiment is not very strong. There is resentment and there is dissatisfaction because of labour conditions, low wages, housing problems, discriminations, and uncertain employment; but their attitude is essentially the same as that of the white American worker feeling economic insecurity. They want to stay "American," and they have no desire for a revolution. Revolutions—in their opinion —are imported by "foreigners" with the exception, of course, of the American Revolution, which was something entirely different. Give them *panem et circenses,* which means a living wage, the sport pages, the comic strips, and now and then a movie or a baseball game, and they are completely satisfied. The same seems true of the Red movements among the share-croppers and labourers in the South, with this difference— they ask only a living wage. Although both black and white workers in America are essentially conservative and "capitalis-tic," racial antagonism still keeps the black and white workers divided. A mixed union still has an artificial character.

Listening in on a conversation between a white train con-ductor and several Negro porters, I heard the conductor com-plaining about "those aliens" who kept wages low. The porters were not much impressed and said: "If you'd had the brains, you would have been a head man by now."

The Negroes fully endorse the American philosophy just as the second-generation Chinese in California do: the fault is not in the system but in the application. It was a revelation to me to hear Negroes sometimes indulge in a glorification of American democracy in the same uncritical way as unsophisti-cated whites often do. Of course, part of this is due to their innate hopefulness, their faith in a bright future. On the other hand, however, they align themselves as far as possible with the wealthier and conservative classes in America because they are afraid that they may lose their jobs at any time on account of their colour, and they are not willing to run the additional risk of being classed as "Red." Without doubt the tradition of better relationships with the better-class whites also plays a role in this attitude which favours adoption of the bourgeois philosophy.

It is only since 1930 that the extreme poverty and misery

have furnished a fertile soil for radicalism among the Negro urban proletariat. The greatest attraction of the communist propaganda, of course, is the unremitting fight against race prejudice. But the skilful utopian appeal of "Gimme that new Communist spirit" which "was good for Comrade Lenin" has not yet been able to defeat "that old-time religion: it's good enough for me." The "communists" are mainly disillusioned unemployed young men and women in their twenties and thirties. Although every emotional issue (Scottsboro case, lynchings, evictions, Italian agression against Ethiopia, etc.) is used to promote the communist cause, since the New Deal communism is decidedly declining: the indirect influence is greater than the direct.

The method of propaganda applied by the communists is essentially the same as that which has been used by a part of the Negro press for a decade or two. A few "smart-aleck" Negroes freed from their "place" by residence in the North have imprinted a stamp of vulgarity and blatancy on certain papers by constantly spitting and growling at white domination and at their own leaders, to the great glee of a race which rejoices at such impudences. It is an expression of the inferiority complex, whereby the Negro public, by way of over-compensation, gains a release from intolerable pressures.

As a matter of fact in some respects Negroes are more American than the Americans. Because of repression of self-determination, and little opportunity to rise to importance, their desire for recognition is confined to the group life. Hence appears a psychopathic tendency towards individualism. Negro society is rent asunder and torn into innumerable factions by senseless jealousies, intrigues, and petty strivings. This lack of coherence and co-operation is a severe impediment to progress. Religion furnishes an outlet for gregarious tendencies but is torn into more bitter sectarian fights than even among whites. In politics race consciousness urges solidarity, but within the Negro community and within the groups of which it is composed discord disrupts unity, and distrust hampers leadership.

They feel themselves Americans and want to be nothing else. But there is the real problem: they are American and Negro. As Negroes they see themselves constantly through American eyes. That unreconciled double-consciousness is their greatest trouble. Africa does not appeal to them at all. An art teacher in one of the southern Negro colleges wished to develop a racial pride in her pupils in order to help them overcome their feeling of inferiority—which as a matter of fact often is pathological and is impressed on their whole bodily appearance and demeanour. Their inability to realize themselves freely has turned back their attention to themselves until their self-consciousness has become entirely out of focus. The teacher, therefore, selected fine pictures of African Negroes, but even these art students could not appreciate them. "These are mere savages," "Their arms are too long," "How far are we from these!" were the reactions. They did not see the manly carriage, the expression of self-assertion which mental freedom and moral independence give. Their standards of evaluation were American. "Going back to Africa" has no attraction for them.

Some teachers, in order to retain the self-esteem necessary for survival and life, try to develop race pride by teaching "Negro history." However, it is clear to the outsider that, although there have been remarkable achievements in some of the Negro civilizations of Africa, these civilizations never can give to the American Negro the inspiration which some of the Asiatic cultures have given to the modern and Western educated youth in which the old heritage still survives. The Negro achievements in sports, prize-fighting, art, literature, and mu-

sic provide a basis on which a sound self-confidence that does
not lapse into racial chauvinism can be built. Negroes have
made original contributions to the arts worthy of pride. In
this field there are tangible evidences of progress and accomplishment. The advantage of the scientific treatment of these
subjects in university classes is that they invite comparison as a
matter of course. Here is needed uncompromising criticism
that is not led astray by a temporary fashion in America and
Europe, and is not afraid of Negro sentiment that stamps such
criticism as "treason to the race."

In my opinion attention is given too exclusively to Negro
problems in most of the Negro colleges and universities. It is
natural; but the danger is—and in my judgment that danger
is not consciously or at least not effectively avoided—that the
Negro problems are not studied in their relativity, in their
world aspect, without which they are apt to increase resentment and not to serve to liberate the mind and the individual-
ity. The only way to mental freedom is analysis. Only in this
way can the pathological self-centredness, resulting from the
oppression psychosis and the repression of self-determination,
and the spell of uniqueness be broken, and the obsession
realized to be the product of general laws.

Although—as far as I can see—a pan-African movement
has no future whatever among the coloured people of America,
their sympathies at this writing are now quite naturally with
the Ethiopians, and the development of the relations between
Italy and Ethiopia is generally and eagerly watched. The
attitude of Japan in this connexion draws special attention. The
modern evolution of Japan is viewed with undisguised sympathy: educated Negroes as a rule are decidedly pro-Japanese.
Their sentiment sometimes goes so far as to express the hope
that some day Japan will administer a severe licking to the
white nations, the United States not excepted. Such statements

should not be taken too seriously. To express emotions is one thing; to act accordingly is another. Negroes are perhaps the most loyal American citizens and the most thoroughly Americanized. In case of national danger they will stand by the American flag as they did during the World War, when German intrigues tried to estrange them.

"Going back to Africa," communism, Japan—none of these offers a solution to the Negro problem. Many Negroes believe that participation in politics will bring it. In order to evaluate this possibility, it is necessary to study a little more closely the composition of the Negro group.

The average American views the Negroes as one unity. Colour barriers and segregation force them to live in one group, separate from the white community. However, within the group there is differentiation, old and new. During slavery the American-born Negroes looked down upon the new importations; the slaves of certain sections regarded themselves as higher and better than outsiders from another state; and the domestic servants of the big planters held themselves far superior even to free persons of colour. After emancipation the latter group and the illegitimate mulatto offspring of provident planters had the advantage over the other freedmen in so far as they had an economic basis from which to start. With them family life gained some stability, whereas property was also a factor in keeping the family together. They formed the nuclei of the higher economic classes which were the first to provide a good education for their children. Apart from this, a certain social stratification developed according to the shades of colour. This distinction is still found in many places where mulatto groups cling together, and intermarriage with dark-skinned outsiders is taboo. Even in Negro colleges groupings among students often "follow the colour line."

In the upper strata differentiation has gone further. Professional groups have emerged, and businessmen have developed. It has been a remarkable evolution. The churches were the first institutions in which self-determination could express itself. From the church one road led to printing establishments because of the need of prayer and hymn books and supplies for the Sunday school; another road led *via* burial associations, undertaking parlours, and insurance companies to banks, which in turn financed Negro stores and other enterprises. Although many white people lent a helpful hand to this development, it is remarkable that the Negroes, without any experience, have built up their economic life even though they were barred from apprenticeship in white institutions. And still the fight is not over. The small Negro stores experience the same difficulties encountered by Japanese and Chinese stores in California. They cater mainly to Negroes. With restricted patronage and little capital, they find great difficulty in competing with the white stores which have larger, more varied, and more attractive supplies. Chain stores make the survival of independent stores especially hard. Other trades suffer because they have not kept pace with the times. City regulations sometimes help white competitors to deprive Negro business of its white patronage, and so on. However, in places with a large Negro population and a coloured group with strong purchasing power, concentrated action of Negro solidarity has not seldom succeeded in exacting courteous service for coloured customers and employment of coloured clerks. Since the importance of the Negro group as a customer has been discovered, there is no reason why, in times to come, the number of coloured people finding employment in white businesses should not increase. Both developments are interesting: the first in making use of segregation as a means for establishing Negro business life, the second by using economic pressure in order to push coloured employees into white businesses. Although the latter are employed only in the coloured sections of the cities, the opening may give the successful ones an opportunity to get ahead.

However this may be, the major portion of these higher classes in the Negro group are still dependent upon the good-will of the whites. Like the share-croppers and tenants who wish to become small farmers, they must be "acceptable." This holds true especially for the professional Negroes, more particularly the teachers. In order to get a job, one has to be "respectable." In this way, there is a pressure which implies submission to the standards of the white group. Leadership in Negro society being in the hands of the higher economic classes, their "respectability" also checks the lower classes. The most outstanding specimen of the "respectable" group is the Negro state college president who, because of his servility and his often wily skill in handling politicians, is despised by northern Negroes as the personification of insincerity and intrigue.

In contrast to this quiet law-abiding group of respectable coloured citizens stands "the bad nigger." He defies "respectability," white supremacy, and police authority. Although he is openly denounced by the "respectable" class and sometimes betrayed by "Uncle Toms," his behaviour is secretly enjoyed. In slavery times he was whipped, sent for correction to a "breaker," or sold "down the river." However, he often escaped to the North where his descendants still live. His numbers there have been increased by the later immigrants from the South who had initiative and energy enough to break away from boll-weevil conditions and enter upon a new unknown urban life as unskilled industrial workers. Out of the slums where they settled a remarkable class of Negro politicians has grown up in recent years which—in collaboration with or in opposition to the white party machines and with the help of hoodlums, gamblers, and bootleggers—has organized the Negro vote in the North in an effective way. In a relatively short time these politicians have managed not only to build up a strategic position in several of the northern states, where they hold the balance of power and actually influence politics in the interests of the Negro, but also to get Negroes placed in the civil service and in offices formerly held by the whites. Their representatives have entered state legislatures and even Congress. These achievements have not failed to impress northern Negro intellectuals and southern coloured students educated in the North. Through the press their successes and their views are broadcast in the South. An increasing number of this younger group is going South to find employment and is gradually beginning to organize what is left of the Negro vote. Undoubtedly there are possibilities, mainly in the cities; but the apathy of the southern Negroes as concerns politics, their acquiescence in their disfranchisement, and the difficulties of registration especially in the states with the "understanding clause" and the white primaries are serious obstacles for the time being. Nevertheless, here and there in the cities (namely, in Memphis, Louisville, Durham, Raleigh, Greensboro, Charlotte, Roanoke, Savannah, Augusta, Atlanta, and the five large Texas cities) the Negro urban vote has already successfully been used in referenda (on tax and bond matters, on the adoption of a city-manager charter, etc.), in non-partisan municipal elections, in "reform" campaigns, and in Presidential elections.

West Virginia, Kentucky, Tennessee, and North Carolina have no state-wide party rule barring Negroes from the Democratic primary. Elsewhere exceptions are sometimes made in favour of individuals. But everywhere registration of Negro voters is restricted. In ordinary state and county elections—with the exception of the border states—the Negro vote is very

small. However, temporary calls on the Negro vote are sometimes made. The largest number of Negroes registered in a
southern state below the border group is Virginia's 18,000—
5.2 per cent of the literate coloured population of voting age
in the state. Alabama, Mississippi, and Lousiana have an almost negligible number of Negro voters. So it will take a
considerable time before the Negro vote in the South will be
able to affect the Negro position in public life. An outsider
who tries to organize the Negro vote is sure to encounter opposition not only from the whites but also from the coloured
people, who fear a recurrence of the disfranchisement campaigns and their associated horrors. The religion of resignation and passive hopefulness preached by the ordinary Negro
minister is also an impediment to new experiments.

"Nobody knows the trouble I see," says a spiritual. "Nobody knows but Jesus." The plantation legend still sets the
pattern.

CHAPTER VI

Negro Education

SOMEWHERE in the South I visited a rural school on a cold winter morning. The building was a poor wooden shack without window-panes. In order to keep out wind and rain, the windows had been stuffed with cardboard. The teacher and the children were not in the school, a fact which was explained on the blackboard, on which I read: "Opened October 15. Closed December 7. Lord, teach us to pray!"

The seventy-six-year-old county superintendent accompanied me on my survey through the county, but had forgotten to tell me that visiting rural schools at that time was not of much use, as a few days before he had closed 34 of his 36 Negro schools. Now he remembered: he had been short of money and had had to reduce his budget; this drastic economy therefore was justified in his opinion. Moreover, he hoped for federal money, and closing the Negro schools would be the right policy to induce the "nigger lovers" in Washington to help him out. In the expectation of that money he had already raised the salaries of his white and coloured teachers, with this difference, that he had (temporarily) dismissed most of his coloured teachers. As a matter of fact the salaries of his coloured teachers had increased from $17 per month to $22 per month, which was exactly $5 more than was paid in the adjoining counties. If the federal money were available, he hoped to establish a five-month school term.

On the same trip I visited a small community of Negro

land-owners. The school teacher, who was at the same time a farmer, was a progressive man. Under his leadership the community had decided to pull down the old dilapidated lodge which housed the school and to build a new, adequate, two-room school, following the Rosenwald plan. When a committee approached the county superintendent for aid, the latter was short of money but gracefully gave them two months of the teacher's salary since, because the old building had been torn down, the children could not go to school. The community contributed the materials for the building and paid the wages of mason and carpenter, but there was no money to pay for plastering the ceiling. The county superintendent therefore was approached once more, whereupon he granted another month of the teacher's salary. "It is an energetic community," he told me.

These unimportant personal experiences are related here because they give a picture of the difficulties Negro education and Negro teachers have to face and of the attitude of a great number of whites.

Edwin R. Embree's *Every Tenth Pupil: The Story of Negro Schools in the South* and Fred McCuistion's *School Money in Black and White*—both publications of the Julius Rosenwald Fund—give the picture in figures. The average expenditure for every pupil throughout the nation in 1930 was $99; the expenditure for white children in the South was $44.31, less than half the national average; the expenditure for Negro children was $12.57, only about one-fourth that for southern white children and about one-eighth that for the average pupil in the nation as a whole. In certain states of the deep South with huge Negro populations, the discrimination is still greater: Georgia spends an average of $35.42 for each white pupil and $6.38 for each Negro; the figures for Mississippi are $45.34 against $5.45. These average figures do not yet tell the whole story because they efface the local differences. In a city like Atlanta a relatively large amount of money is spent on Negro education, which increases the state average, but it must be kept in mind that in many of the rural counties much less than $6.38 per Negro pupil is being spent.

The difference between the national average and the average for the southern states finds explanation in the fact that the South is poor as compared with the rest of the United States. The divergence between the expenditure per white and that per Negro pupil in the South is caused primarily by the difference in the salaries of the white and the coloured teachers, and secondarily by the progress that consolidation of schools has made in the case of the white schools, as a consequence of which free transportation of pupils to the consolidated schools greatly increases educational expense. Further causes of the discrepancy are shorter terms for Negro schools and the difference in the value of school plant and equipment—Negro schools often being taught in churches, lodges, and dilapidated shacks, with textbooks lacking and furniture improvised.

The lower salaries influence the quality and competency of the teachers. Nevertheless, the same curriculum is taught in the Negro schools as in the white, and the same books are supposed to be used. The children are grouped in grades, but, as a matter of fact, these grades have only a theoretical value which does not correspond with that which the white schools attach to it. I found pupils in an eighth grade studying commercial geography without maps, and in another place I found them studying the state history. In both cases they understood almost nothing of the subjects, with the result that the geography and history classes simply developed into very poor reading classes—poor because the worst kind of training in reading is the reciting of words and sentences which have no meaning for the reader. I have seen textbooks on literature used when the pupils did not understand one word of what they read. The English was far too difficult. I found seventh- and eighth-grade pupils unable to spell "April" or "cotton."

The rural schools with their inadequate buildings, poorly paid and poorly prepared teachers, low standards (fictitious grades), poor attendance, and insufficient equipment reflect exactly the attitude sketched in the previous chapter.

Nevertheless, there is a great improvement as compared with what has been. Before the Civil War there existed practically no public system of education in most of the southern states. It is to the merit of the reconstruction governments that they stressed this point, but the "poor whites" profited more than the Negroes. It is a wonder that, after the undoing of reconstruction, any sort of education for the Negro was maintained. The exasperation of the whites was great, and the impoverishment and indebtedness of the southern states was greater. Several states had not recovered by 1900. Thus Negro education would have been neglected altogether if the missionary spirit of the denominational groups, particularly northern men and women, had not come to the rescue.

The next great factor in the history of Negro education in the South was the Jeanes teachers, about whom we shall say a few words later on. Then came Thomas Jesse Jones's re-remarkable survey, *Negro Education in the United States* (1917), which gave a thorough and sorrowful picture of the existing conditions; this was a great stimulus to improvement. The General Education Board, established by John D. Rockefeller in 1903, provided the funds for the appointment of the state agents for Negro schools, which gave Negro education an organic place in the state departments. The next step was the county training schools, providing for better teachers and preparing the way for Negro secondary education. Julius Rosenwald's generosity found in S. L. Smith the man to

promote a huge school-building programme which stimulated
co-operation between Negro self-interest, white philanthropy,
and the administrators of public funds. It made public officials
aware of a neglected task; it stirred up the whites to do something also for the white rural schools, which could not stay behind the Negro schools; and it awakened Negro interest,
pride, and community feeling. There are now more than five
thousand Rosenwald schools in the South. Of recent years,
perhaps, the pace has been a little too fast: the aspect of some
of the schools does not always give evidence of the interest
which one would expect; and some schools have proved to
be situated in the wrong places. But as a whole, Mr. Rosenwald's initiative has had results better than could have been
expected. As soon as a new Rosenwald building has arisen,
more pupils have been enlisted than was dreamed of before;
there has been better attendance; the county superintendent
has felt obliged to do his share, provide better qualified teachers, pay better salaries, give better equipment, prolong the
school term, and, as the pupils stayed longer in school, add
more grades; the quality of the instruction and the standards
have improved.

The last but not the least factor of importance in the history
of Negro education in the South was the improvement in the
economic situation, which made more money available. North
Carolina took the lead. Its economy was not based on cotton
alone. Tobacco became more and more significant, especially
after the boll-weevil had invaded the cotton areas. Moreover,
flourishing industries developed which not only strengthened
public funds but also introduced a new spirit, more inclined to
give the Negro his share. Finally, North Carolina was blessed
with fine leadership. Governor Charles B. Aycock, who came
to power as a result of Negro disfranchisement, was at the
same time the champion of Negro education, for which he

fought against all narrow prejudice. His example was followed by his successors, assisted by men of vision in the department of education and the state university.[1]

After the World War, and especially during the period of great prosperity (1923–29) when not only the nation but the whole world was feverishly expanding its secondary education, this movement also took hold of the South. The Negro, too, profited by it. In rapid succession Negro high schools arose all over the South.

Everyone who has seen a little deeper than the surface, however, understands that this remarkable growth was not altogether a spontaneous development. For the most part it was the work of the state agents for Negro schools, who emphasized the needs and grasped the opportunities. Nobody who has not actually seen them in their work can realize the difficulties they must face almost daily. Although nominally officers of the state departments of education, their salaries are paid by the philanthropic foundations; they are supervisors of Negro education but have no authority whatever. For their success they must depend entirely upon the goodwill they manage to create and upon their personal prestige. They live and work in the South with its prejudices. Of course they are Southerners themselves and know how far they can go, but they are restrained in their efforts by the milieu. They have to be extremely careful not to arouse sentiments that

---

[1] No record of social forces in the South is complete without some reference to the University of North Carolina. For many years it has been one of the very few institutions of higher learning in the whole section which has approached national standards in scholarship. Especially distinguished is the university's Institute for Research in Social Science under the leadership of Dr. Howard Odum and a brilliant and courageous group of associates. This Institute has dared to study and write freely of social problems, including those of the Negro and race relations. These studies have been published and given wide distribution through the eminent—and equally courageous—University of North Carolina Press.

would impede the progress of their work. For their success they must depend upon the traditional paternalistic attitude towards the Negro who keeps in his place. They have a definite task, but they are subordinate to the state superintendent of education, who may be an educator and an organizer, but who may also be a politician, playing partisan politics. In the latter case it may be that the state superintendent of education does not hold any academic degree and is personally affiliated with an institution that *sells* degrees, or that he expects the officers of his department who wish to keep their jobs to contribute part of their salaries for some unknown purpose. Sometimes the discrepancy between the costs connected with his periodical election, which he has to pay himself, and the actual amount of his salary suggests motives other than merely educational for his choice of this particular function. It can easily be imagined what interest such a state superintendent has in Negro education, especially if the next election is in sight. Federal money for unemployed Negro teachers may be spent for white teachers who, contrary to sacred southern traditions, will even be given employment in Negro schools. The same holds true for a state superintendent, appointee of a governor-politician, who has to obey the whims of his master. The governor is often the determining factor so far as the amount of state appropriations is concerned. He may dismiss college presidents and university professors to replace them with political friends. He may hold the view that a five-month school term is sufficient for anybody, or that there is no need for supervision, or that in a consolidated school system free transportation is a luxury.

In the state department of education, the agent for Negro schools has to awaken the interest of his fellow-officers working in the field of white education. He may or may not succeed in gaining their co-operation, which is of the greatest importance

as regards appropriations, curriculum studies, setting of standards, rating, teacher-training programmes, and so on. Instead
of co-operation, he may encounter contempt of his job. His
colleagues do not need him for their work; he needs them for
his, and he cannot demand their attention.

The greatest difficulties of the state agent for Negro schools,
however, are formed by the contacts with the county superintendents whom he must approach for new school buildings,
repairs of the old buildings, additional grades, more equipment, better salaries for the Negro teachers, better qualified
teachers, appointment of a Jeanes teacher, or a longer school
term. Being elected by popular vote, the county superintendent
is fairly representative of the feelings of his community, and
dependent upon his constituents for his job. Sometimes he is
just a politician who has no interest whatever in Negro education nor even in white education except as it is a means of his
holding a job. After several vain efforts, the state agent will
leave him alone, hoping for better times. This means that for
several years nothing is being done for Negro education in
this community. Sometimes with the help of the local Negroes,
who arrange a dinner in the school for the white folks and
know how to create goodwill, the state agent will succeed.
Introduction of domestic science in the school programme will
be advocated by the trustees as a means of making better cooks,
vocational agriculture as a guarantee for keeping the Negro
in his place. Sometimes the state agent will be able to awaken
the interest of the county school board or of some influential
white man in the community, and in this way break the resistance or the indifference of the county superintendent. Sometimes by his constant insistence he will wear out the unwilling
superintendent; sometimes the professional pride of the
county superintendent who wants to show results will give
the agent the opportunity to achieve his end. If the county

superintendent is willing to co-operate, the fact that the state agent is at the same time the representative of the philanthropic foundations and therefore can influence their gifts can be a great help. The state agent has to build up his influence gradually; he must be a judge of human nature and know how to handle these rural authorities, the cheerful ones, the pompous ones, the wicked ones. He must have tact; he must have patience. If in a certain county he has made progress by gaining the confidence of the county superintendent, this officer may die or not be re-elected; then the state agent must start afresh. Other difficulties arise: when the county superintendent has to reduce his budget, it is the line of least resistance to find the economies in the field of Negro education.

I give this outline of the difficulties of the state agent not so much because of the importance of this officer in the whole of Negro education as to emphasize the lack of organization and the character of the obstacles in the way of establishing a better system. The governor is a politician dependent for his election on the vote of his constituents, the white electorate. The same holds true, in most of the cases, of the state superintendent. Other factors besides education determine the election. In the preceding chapter, it was reported how the Negro spectre still rules the South and how common Negro-baiting still is in the game of politics. However, the real power in educational matters is still in the hands of the local authorities, who allocate the money to be spent for education. They levy the local taxes and distribute the state appropriations. Again, they are elected by popular vote and are dependent on public opinion. The electorate is white, and has a natural aversion to taxes and very little interest in Negro education. These factors must be taken into account by the county superintendent and the county board of education. The result is that, although there is some sort and some amount of Negro education everywhere, Negro education still does not have a fixed, legitimate, acknowledged place. It is realized that something must be done in order to keep the Negro satisfied and in order to uphold the American slogan of free schools for every child, but it is rare that a community has any real interest in planning or building a wise system of education for the race. Politically, it is not generally admitted that the Negro has a right to schools or to other public services. This attitude again is in accordance with what was stated in the fifth chapter. The Negro is still not recognized as a citizen despite the Civil War amendments.

Because of this situation, it is very hard to draw up a programme and to execute it. As a matter of fact, here lies the weakest point of the whole educational system, not only coloured but also white. The over-decentralization is a survival of the frontier period, when the parents in a neighbourhood had to provide for the education of their children. Prevailing public opinion placed the responsibility for the education of the children upon the parents alone. It was opposed to public taxation as a means of universal education. Today, public opinion holds that every child should have an opportunity to attend school at public expense. But the whole county government, with its elected judge, prehistoric jail conditions, and medieval sheriff, still belongs to the ox-cart and buggy era. In a state like Arkansas, which, since it abolished the office of county superintendent (1933), has invested all educational authority in the numerous district boards, the situation is still worse.

Of course, the freedom resulting from local control has had its good aspects as well. Experiments undertaken by communities which were interested in improving public schools undoubtedly have effected notable enlargements of the educational programme; their examples have, in course of time, advanced the cause of education. On the other hand such instances are relatively rare, whereas in the majority of cases local narrowness has been an obstacle to general progress. Moreover, egotism has played a great role in the delimitation of the school districts: cliques have been eager to preserve the taxes for themselves, inconsiderate of less fortunate neighbours. So in the wealthy districts (counties, cities) one sees a luxurious system flourishing, while in the adjoining area incredible conditions prevail. It has been a conflict between individualism and a real democracy "by the people, *for* the people." The depression that began in 1929 has had this good side: it has made clear the impossibility of this kind of "organization."

Some state influence has regularly existed. The common forms of state supervision were requirement of reports, inspection, and the giving of advice, often by means of state-wide conferences. In some cases the state department was entitled to issue orders to review local action, or to withhold payments of salary, but this was infrequent. Some states introduced exclusive state certification of teachers; state supervision over teacher training was expanding. Accrediting of schools, a form of recognition which implies capacity to enforce improvements, was falling into the hands of state departments. Control of the curricula by state departments had also been extended to a marked degree. In short, state supervision over local schools was becoming more extensive and intensive, with the general object of raising standards and securing a greater degree of uniformity in the minimum curriculum and equipment. However, so strong was the sentiment which recognized education as an enterprise which should be kept "close to the people" that state departments on the whole were not adequately staffed to provide more than routine services to the school districts of the state. The granting of aid from state funds to local districts was common practice in almost all states, but the county school boards were practically free to spend the money in the way they thought best. The tendency appeared, however, to use the grants to localities for the enforcement of standards upon the local school authorities. In some states an equalization fund was created to help the weak districts with additional appropriations in order to equalize educational opportunities, but neither in length of school term nor in quantity and quality of instruction could equality be effected since the counties and school districts varied so greatly in economic and financial strength.

Then the depression came. Some counties were unable to collect their taxes and were operating on money borrowed against uncollected taxes. Some could not even borrow money and paid their teachers in scrip, or hurriedly closed their schools. Practically everywhere the necessity for state help was felt.

North Carolina introduced the new principle that the state itself is primarily responsible for the support and maintenance of the six-month school term in every district demanded in the state constitution. It has, therefore, undertaken to finance the whole cost out of its own revenues according to state standards of costs. Public education, as North Carolina sees it, is not only a state function over which the state (while delegating it to the counties as the administrative agencies of the state) will exercise some general control, but it is also a solemn state obligation which the state must discharge with all the resources at its command.

This idea is gaining ground, and when it is generally accepted, conditions in the rural schools cannot but improve. It implies that the state will not only set the standards for the qualification of teachers and for the instruction given, but also guarantee the salaries of the teachers according to attendance and teaching load. This means that the state appropriations

will no longer be given on the basis of a theoretical number of
educables but will be given on the basis of pupils actually in
school and of teachers actually teaching. It excludes the possibility that county school boards can manipulate state money
according to their whims. Another source of economy will be
rationalization of the distribution of educational opportunity.
No teachers need be allotted to a school operated in close
proximity to another school of the same type. Some states have
already begun to introduce these novelties.

The greatest advantage of the new development of state
control of education is that it removes education from the
sphere of local partisanships, sentiments, and prejudices. In
some states steps have already been taken in that direction.
Here and there the state superintendent of education, elected
by popular vote, is replaced by a state commissioner appointed
by the state board of education. This last form of appointment
is to be preferred to that by the governor as ratified by the state
legislature, for educational interests are safer in the hands of
the board. In the same way some states have abolished the
popular election of the county superintendent; he is appointed
by the county school board, standards of eligibility being set by
the state board of education for the purpose of safeguarding
competency. There is no objection when the county school
board or even the district trustees appoint the teachers, as long
as the state board of education in co-operation with the state
department fixes the indispensable qualifications.

The picture sketched in the previous paragraphs does not
represent the present reality but is composed of tendencies already actually existing. However, it will be a long time before
local sentiments, interest groups, and petty ambitions, which
are the main obstacles to the natural development of sound
tendencies, will be overcome.

The growing influence of the state also opens the way to

planning in the educational field, which up until now has been practically lacking. Many people hold that no planning is necessary in the educational field. They claim that everybody has the right to be educated not only through elementary school and high school but also through college. They claim that America is a democracy which in order to realize its ideals is dependent upon fully educated citizens and voters. Moreover, "a unique characteristic of the American social system which has been of importance in determining the development of American education is the freedom of individual choice of occupations. In this country a boy or girl is free to follow his or her personal bent in the choice of an occupation. There are no social barriers to prevent any individual from entering any vocation. The educational system is, accordingly, at liberty to arrange the education of its wards in keeping with their individual abilities." Further, it is also claimed that the situation here is different from that of many countries of the Old World in this sense—that certain industries do not admit labourers under twenty years of age. In order to compensate for the tendency to close industry to children, society must provide new means of protecting them and of profitably occupying their time.

Others hold that "my cook has the same right as I to enjoy Shakespeare in her spare time, and education in this country must enable her to do so." Again, others point out that the American school must assume tasks formerly performed by the family. Besides, modern educational theories demand more attention for the individual child, demand its right to be educated according to its abilities. "The school for the child; not the child for the school." "The pupil must be happy." The children must enjoy more years of exemption from the responsibilities of self-support than have been granted to the former generation. Industry restricts the working hours of its labourers, invents labour-saving devices. This means more leisure: the new slogan is born—"education for leisure."

All these wishes and claims suggest a permanent and unlimited availability of funds for educational purposes, and only one yardstick—the individual desire which must be satisfied. However, the following are the facts for the South: There still are "social barriers" preventing an individual from "entering any vocation," and child labour is still fairly general. As to educational opportunities, they are so limited for the great mass of the people that talk about "education for leisure" and "everybody has the right to a free college education" sounds like bitter irony; the southern states are very poor, can spend only a limited amount of money on education, and intentionally restrict appropriations for Negro education.

Under these circumstances common sense would command that high-sounding theories be left aside for the moment, and an urgency and emergency programme be framed. Such a plan does not now exist anywhere in Negro education.

For instance, the development of secondary education for Negroes after the World War was based merely upon the individual's desire for higher education, not upon any specific reflection of social needs and possibilities. It was effected by sacrificing quality to quantity; high schools arose before competent teachers were available. The result was that *all* the institutions giving instruction beyond high school became teacher-training institutions. Graduates were sure to find jobs in the increasing number of high schools. However, that increase has come to an end since the depression and is not likely to be resumed at the same pace in the near future. Consequently the number of places for college graduates is limited, whereas the stream of students seeking improvement of their economic conditions has not declined. It is even likely to increase because of the greater number of accredited high schools which send graduates to college. At the present time, some of these college graduates have found employment in the elementary schools, but here there is also a limit. In the first place it is questionable whether these college graduates are the right type of teachers for the rural school; and in the second place the salaries are so small in some states that only local girls can be employed; and, finally, many of the local authorities prefer local teachers and are prejudiced against college-bred Negroes.

Although the birth-rate among the educated classes of the Negro group is so low that newcomers are needed in order to fill the ranks, the economic possibilities remain restricted. Due to the New Deal, the present situation is not normal since the money provided by the different federal alphabetical agencies actually creates employment for and stimulates the training of social workers and agricultural students, and has even led to the expansion of institutions. It is extremely doubtful what will become of these people when these crisis organizations have disappeared.

Therefore, the problem for the near future will be how to engage these Negro college graduates in useful occupations. As a result of the existing prejudice, the openings for Negroes in the professional field are few. In the first chapter the same fact was stated in connexion with the Chinese in California. Only the unusually capable man will succeed in breaking the wall of prejudice.

It must be acknowledged that very few Negro colleges (and universities) can stand a comparison with the better white institutions; there are only a few first-class scholars among the numerous Negro professors, and standards are lowered by the absence of a sound selection at entrance. This holds true for many white institutions as well, but their graduates are not handicapped by the existing prejudice. The conclusion would seem to be that, in the years to come, special effort should be made to effectuate a rigorous selection of pupils for the higher institutions and to bring about a radical revision and a deliberate, systematic improvement of the teaching staff. This will be a difficult task, as the foundations and white philanthropists who used to contribute liberally in the past have been badly hit by the depression and must honour the draft of New Deal expenditure. This enhances the possibility of lowering instead of raising the requirements for admission. However, another solution is possible. There are too many institutions for higher learning, many of them with a rather low standing. Some have not survived the depression; others just manage to keep alive, to the detriment of any reasonable standard of instruction. Fewer as well as better colleges for Negroes are clearly indicated.

Co-operation and a reconsideration of the situation are needed. Although some hopeful beginnings have been made, they must develop on a larger scale in order to establish rational economies and to spend the available funds in the most profitable way.

Apart from selection and rationalization of educational opportunities, sound early education is necessary. Many Negro students have grown up under very restricted and depressed conditions in which there was little opportunity for personal development or acquisition of the rudiments of decent living. Although the better classes of the Negro group as a rule conform to the standards of family life in the white community, it is a well-known fact that, as a survival from slavery times and due to the great percentage of illegitimacy and desertion in the rural South and in the cities, family life among Negroes finds its centre in the hard-working mother who has little time to spare for the guidance of her children. The segregation of the Negro community excludes contacts with the white society and often means cultural impoverishment, because the stimuli of the milieu which forcibly brings together all the elements of Negro society, including the most undesirable ones, are not always likely to develop the best traits in human nature. The result is that boys and girls come to school and college without the home training which is indispensable to them if they hope afterwards to form helpful contacts with white society. Many conflicts could have been avoided if the language of social intercourse had been learned.

Lack of planning also influences the trend of elementary and secondary education for Negroes. I already pointed out that as a rule the state departments of education make up the curricula. Although the county boards of education and even the local school district trustees have the right to do so, they are lacking in competency and gladly follow the suggestions of the state department. The result is a tendency to uniformity which is strengthened by the general trend towards consolidation. Since the World War great efforts have been made to consolidate the white schools in the different counties. Free transportation brings the rural children together in a limited number of huge town schools. Rural schools with poor equipment, often overcrowded conditions, and poor teachers were mostly very inefficient. From an educational point of view consolidation has brought great improvement as compared with the conditions which previously existed. In other respects, however, consolidation is subject to criticism. In the first place the great building programme connected with it has increased indebtedness, and transportation has enhanced the costs, which are now a heavy burden on the local taxpayers. In the second place the tendency towards uniformity has been strengthened, since the requirements for admission to college dominate the subject matter. Sometimes the states fix the standards; sometimes other accrediting agencies determine the direction of the instruction. Another important factor in the trend towards uniformity is the textbooks, which do not take into account the local diversity. All these circumstances serve to establish a programme which is based essentially on urban needs. From a sociological standpoint, such a programme was justified to a certain extent by the great urbanization movement in the years of prosperity, the rapid industrialization of the country, the depressed conditions of agriculture, and the greater economic possibilities in the cities. However, in this way the school educated the children away from the rural areas which in fact were drained of their intellect. Although the curriculum studies made during the last years in several of the southern states under the direction of Peabody College include much "progressive" phraseology, they are still under the spell of the urbanization movement. No attention is paid to the difference between rural and urban conditions. The studies lack sociological foundation.

The most encouraging sign in the rural area is the Council on Rural Education recently created by the Julius Rosenwald Fund. This movement looks towards a reorganization of rural education on the basis of rural needs. Concentrating on the South, it very properly (and necessarily) is not confining its efforts to a single race, but is considering the problems of rural education for all the people.

In the last chapter an attempt will be made to answer the question, whether basic economic conditions as revealed by the depression still justify this disregard of an adaption of the school to the needs of the milieu. It is sufficient to state here that even before the depression only some of the high-school graduates went to college, which means that the vital interests of the majority were sacrificed to those of the few. The doctrine of "equality of opportunity" was interpreted to mean that all must be given the chance to go to college; it really meant a restriction of diversification, a restriction of "the right to individual development according to abilities."

In this educational scheme no special attention was paid to Negro education. Negro schools followed more or less the course of studies of the white schools, so far as qualifications of teachers and general equipment allowed. The Negroes, afraid of discrimination, wanted exactly the same education as the whites as far as they could get it and were *a priori* opposed to a programme which would differentiate between Negro and white education. However, apart from the usual discrimination which resulted from the unwillingness to spend the same amount of money on Negro education as on white, discrimination existed in this sense. Certain types of training were intentionally withheld from the Negroes. This is especially true for the vocational field, which, while offering a means of keeping the Negro in his place as a worker, introduced possibilities of competition intolerable to the (white) organized labour groups.

All these factors together have affected Negro education in a very serious way. Financial restrictions impeded the execution of a programme which was beyond reach. Less inspiring environment, poorer equipment, less qualified teachers, heavier teacher-load, and shorter school terms were the main obstacles, whereas the programme itself was not adapted to the specific needs of Negro society. The result was that basic requirements often were neglected. Although the language difficulties for Negro pupils are greater than for the white, no special attention was given to fundamentals such as reading and spelling. The same textbooks are used as in the corresponding grades of the white schools, regardless of the fact that the Negro pupils cannot understand them.

The same objections can be made against the teacher-training institutions. Too little attention is paid to the difficulties that the average rural Negro teacher must face. On the contrary, in several Negro colleges and universities there is the tendency to imitate certain exclusive white institutions; as concerns teacher training, the example of Peabody College is accepted as standard. Emphasis is placed on laboratory and demonstration schools, but practice teaching is neglected. Other institutions use excellently equipped schools for a limited amount of practice teaching, which does not prepare for the rural schools with short terms and practically no equipment. Elaborate courses are given in curriculum making, but the state curriculum and its applications to the rural conditions (short school-terms, seven or eight grades under one teacher, irregular attendance, admission of pupils at any time during the school year, etc.) are not studied. A happy exception is found in the Forsyth Normal School in Georgia, where an interesting experiment is going on. Not only is attention paid to practice teaching in an average rural school, but also the local teachers are given special courses, while the students of the normal school replace them in their local schools under supervision of the personnel of the normal school.

Another indication and another cause of the lack of planning in education is the absence of a proper co-ordination between the several agencies occupied with aspects of the educational problem. In the first place there is overlapping between the farm-demonstration agent, who is subordinate to the Department of Agriculture, and the agricultural teacher (the Smith-Hughes man), who is under the Office of Education in the Department of the Interior. It must be admitted that, in the days when no instruction in agriculture was given, the farm-demonstration agents performed a useful task. Since the number of Smith-Hughes men has been increased, the need for continuation of the farm-demonstration agents would be doubtful, were it not that in the past two years the latter have been engrossed with Agricultural Adjustment Administration work. Although some theoretical division of labour between the two government agencies has been established, skilful publicity of the successes of farm-demonstration work cannot obscure the fact that duplication exists in practice. Similar overlappings take place between the home-demonstration agent, the county social-worker, the county nurse, the Jeanes teacher, and the active domestic-science teacher who does not restrict her task to the classroom but does follow-up work, often with excellent results, in the homes of her pupils. Here again the lack of co-operation and co-ordination is due to the severalty of the bodies to which these agents belong. Personal relationships between the leaders may bring about a local solution, but such a solution is achieved despite the system.

Special mention should here be made of the Jeanes teacher. Although she has no definite task, she has been a great factor in the organization and the improvement of Negro education. Fostered and in part financed by one of the philanthropic foundations, the Anna T. Jeanes Fund, she is a special Negro assistant to the county superintendent, who, in co-operation with the state agent for Negro schools, directs her work. Sometimes she is a community worker and endeavours to build up community interest not only in education but also in improved living conditions. Sometimes she is an attendance officer; sometimes she is used for administrative work. Perhaps her greatest contribution has been as a supervisor and guide of the Negro teachers. The difference between counties where a Jeanes teacher is working and those where such an officer is not employed is striking, the more so because very few county superintendents or their assistants give any guidance to their Negro teachers. Where relations between county superintendent and the Jeanes teacher are good, this officer can also influence the selection of the teaching staff and thereby gradually improve the quality of education.

Incidental federal interference in educational matters during the present economic emergency causes other inconsistencies. Here and there it creates a nursery school for a small group of children; the teacher must go out herself to induce the parents to surrender their children. It creates adult classes in places where there is only little interest on the part of the adults. I cannot regard it as a great loss if the two eighty-year-old Negro women whom I found spelling the first-grade reader had never accomplished this remarkable achievement during their lifetimes. Such things happen in counties where all available money should be concentrated on the primary needs of primary education. The teachers had been unemployed because they were poor teachers; now they not only had jobs, easier jobs than in the public schools, but they got the salaries of white teachers, for the Federal Government does not discriminate.

Of course the money was given for a special purpose. Naturally, it cannot be spent for a more urgent purpose. It was given because the Federal Government must be impartial and believes that what is necessary for New York does no harm somewhere deep in the rural South, to which Washington is almost as legendary as is Europe.

Meanwhile, the Federal Government could do much more for national education by creating a federal equalization fund. However, here the sensitive issue of states' rights and of the extension of federal control enters the picture. Meanwhile, it would be desirable if a solution for this question could be found which would safeguard the right of the states to outline their own programmes, but which at the same time would open the possibility of equalizing educational opportunities in the country, with the understanding that federal appropriations should be given only for well-defined objects and under such conditions that a real equalization of opportunity for all the citizens could be brought about.

In the last analysis the lack of planning in Negro education is due to the fundamental problem of the Negro. Although there still are people who regard all Negro education as nonsense, the majority will not deny it to the coloured man. But what education? Academic instruction? Little use. Vocational training? That spells competition, conflict! What is feared is the change of status. The Negro should keep in his place. Negro progress is more feared than his criminality.

An old southern senator, a perfect gentleman of the old school, a provident master for "his people," told me of the following occurrence. In a certain county—after the erection of a white high school had been stopped by the unwillingness of the whites to contribute 50 per cent of the costs of the building when the state offered to pay the other 50 per cent—the Negroes got together and sent a deputation to the state department of education, asking whether the same offer would be made in the case of a Negro high school. A few days after the affirmative answer was received, the Negroes deposited their share at the bank. In that county there is now a Negro high school but no white high school.

The reaction of the senator was sympathy, tempered with fear. He saw clearly that the graduates would not stay in the county: their parents' work would not satisfy them. There also would be the danger of a transgression of the colour line, and that would spell conflict and blood. Sorrowfully he quoted the concluding sentences of André Siegfried's discussion of the Negro problem: [2]

---

[2] In *America Comes of Age*, p. 108 (1927). The original French text of the last paragraph reads:

"Ainsi, de quelque côté qu'on se tourne, la solution échappe, et tout aussi

Is the régime of yesterday and today to carry on?

"Yes," replies the South; "nothing else is possible!"

Why not suppress the insults, recognize the Negro as a man, but maintain the separation of the races?

"No!" answers the horror-stricken South. "This very contempt is the best possible barrier, and once this line of defence has been pierced, we should have a hideous confusion."

No matter which way we turn in the North or the South, there seems to be no solution. The colour problem is an abyss into which we can look only with terror.

bien au Nord qu'au Sud. Ce problème est un gouffre, sur lequel on ne peut se pencher sans effroi, et *où la race supérieure elle-même risque de perdre quelque chose de sa dignité.*" Les Etats-Unis d'aujourd'hui, p. 103 (1927). A translation of the final sentence is: "The colour problem is an abyss into which we can look only with terror and *in which the superior race itself is risking the loss of part of its dignity.*" The italics are mine.

CHAPTER VII

Prejudice or Progress

THE rural South is still at the mercy and whim of King Cotton. However, the famous "billion-dollar cotton crop" is an accomplishment fraught with complications. The South produces roughly one-half of the cotton of the world; the rest is grown in other countries, such as Egypt, India, China, the Soviet Union, and Brazil—countries with a very low standard of living. The experience of the last years has shown that cotton production outside of the United States is increasing. The result is that, aside from the demand, not America but the conditions in those other parts of the world determine the cotton price.

This price is such that cotton cannot pay wages but must be produced on shares. "If the average cotton crop were produced by man labour working at an average rate of wages, it would have to sell for fully twice the price now received in order to pay out." This statement of 1926 still holds true.

The solution would be mechanization—as has been the case with rice, which is now profitably grown in Texas in competition with the low-cost rice-growing regions outside of America. Mechanization would reduce the cost of producing cotton and thus enable the United States to compete more advantageously with those foreign nations which might cling to hand labour. Mechanical pickers would displace much of the hand labour now in use.

However, the way in which cotton still is produced has not

changed in most places during the last century. Cotton production requires much labour, especially in the chopping and picking season. This means—in connexion with the cotton price —that labourers are required to work for a payment in subsistence, with the terms of remuneration set without the wage market, a problem that can be solved only through child and woman labour. Therefore, tenants with large families are preferred to unmarried men, since the labour force of the family determines its cotton acreage, its income, and the advances obtainable for living expenses on the security of its interests in the crop.

The second factor which, aside from weather and weevil, determines the income of the tenant is the fertility of the soil. In South Carolina where one-fourth or one-third of the total value of the crop must be spent for fertilizers, the earnings are less than in Texas where the soil is not so worn out as it is in the older cotton-growing regions. In those regions the income is also depressed by the fact that, since in Texas the relatively flat land is favourable to the use of tractors and allows some mechanization, the cost of hand labour is 50 per cent higher than in Texas.

The third factor which influences the actual income of the producer is the lack of operating capital, which causes the tenant or small holder to depend on the advances of the merchant, fertilizer company, or landlord. For his farm and household supplies, the tenant has to pay with his crop. Not only are the time charges higher than the cash price, but he has also to pay the interest on the credit furnished. This means that, despite anti-usury laws, he must pay a total interest of 25 to 60 and more per cent yearly. On the one hand, this is an indication of the helplessness of the tenants and share-croppers; on the other hand, it is an evidence of their extreme poverty and of the great risks involved in the transaction—risks not only because of the fluctuations of the cotton price but also because of the inefficiencies of the system and the irresponsibility of the tenants.

About 90 per cent of the cotton labourers have been working and are still working under such circumstances. No wonder that many never get out of debt, and that the crop lien system has the same effect as peonage. However, recent studies in Georgia and North Carolina have shown that in many cases tenants were better off than small land-owners since the latter had also to pay in cash not only the interest on their mortgages but also the taxes, which were higher than the rent due from the tenants. Sometimes the landlord, not dependent on the plantation for his income and bound by sentimental ties to the land and its tenants, the descendants of former slaves, charges only a nominal rent.

Since the majority of the rural population is living under the circumstances outlined above, the low cost of cotton production in the South cannot be regarded as socially advantageous. The resulting social damage is paid for by criminality, poor education, and the like, while the small remuneration for agricultural toil keeps the wages in the cotton mills low and drags down the whole society.

The Federal Government has tried to improve this situation by means of the Agricultural Adjustment Act. The A.A.A. is not a development arising wholly out of the depression; it is the outcome of a series of efforts to secure new agricultural reform legislation, beginning in the post-war years and including the experimentation carried on under the Federal Farm Board. It is the outcome of several lines of development: a production adjustment movement, the first form of which was the outlook programme; a marketing adjustment movement, of which the Agricultural Marketing Act was one phase; and a land-use control movement. The significance of the Agricultural Adjustment Act and its permanent value lie not so much in its price-raising and emergency relief features and the loan policy connected with it, as in its contribution to a continuing programme of improved agricultural organization for production, marketing, and land use.

Limitation of the total amount of cultivated land, and agricultural diversification, with its restriction of the cotton acreage, mean less employment of hand labour. Reduction of the crop also affects employment in the transportation field (railways, etc.), in the cotton gins, in the fuel-producing industries, and the like.

A sound land-use programme in connexion with a crop and acreage-restriction programme cannot permanently content itself with acreage reduction percentages which apply to the whole cotton-producing area; it must retain in production those areas where cotton is grown most profitably, and take out of production other regions where production costs are high. A policy of this kind is inevitable in the case of an export commodity of a highly competitive nature. This means a further westward shift of the American cotton belt. Texas already produces a third of the nation's crop; in New Mexico, Arizona, and southern California cotton culture is developing. Such a rationalization of production would bring profound agricultural and social changes to the older cotton states. Meanwhile, the absolute rule of King Cotton is no longer unchallenged. Aside from rayon, which competes with cotton as well as with silk, several new cotton substitutes have been developed from cellulose made of wood pulp and are replacing an increasing percentage of the world cotton consumption.

Changes in the international textile situation also threaten southern cotton growers. The shift of cotton mills from Europe to the East—primarily from Great Britain, Germany, and the Netherlands to Japan, India, and China—has made great headway in the past five years; and this shift has affected the foreign demand for American cotton. In other cotton-producing countries, such as the Soviet Union, Egypt, Brazil, Argentina, and Peru, there is also a noticeable tendency to develop their own textile industries. The principal effect of this trend is that the great exporters of cotton cloth woven of the American staple will lose their foreign outlets. The new industries in the Orient have developed techniques for using the locally grown short-staple lengths instead of the medium-staple cotton of which the United States produced 80 per cent of the world's supply and which was used in the British mills. Although Japan, in her recent bid for foreign markets, has used proportionately more American cotton as Great Britain has used less, Japan is now promoting cotton culture in Manchukuo, China, and elsewhere in order to make herself independent of the American market. International trade in both raw cotton and cotton cloth will be diminished to the disadvantage of the United States. Even if this were not the case, the practically unchanged American tariff policy can hardly avoid bringing disaster to the cotton producers since the European nations will lack the means to pay for the American exports.

From whichever side we approach this question, the indications are for a future in which fewer people—white and black—will be employed in the cultivation of cotton, with the possibility that in great parts of the classic cotton-growing area cotton will have to be abandoned altogether. From a social viewpoint this will mean no great loss, if only a better form of profitable employment can be found for those people who are now working under peonage conditions. Emergency relief measures help out for the moment, but such a dark future requires long-range planning.

Although southern states bound by pre-depression tenden-

cies are basing their educational programme on the expectation of increased urbanization, it is very improbable that
developments will take that direction. Industrialization, which
was the cause of the urbanization movement, seems to have
reached its zenith.

The period of prosperity represented recovery from the
severe business depression of 1921, but was, to an even
greater extent, due to the requirements for the economic reconstruction of Europe, which meant a large demand for
American products. The rise of the United States, in the
years since the World War, as the most important creditor
nation of the world (presumably supplied with inexhaustible
funds of credit for foreign investment), combined with a
willingness to lend freely to the countries of Europe and
other continents, led to extensive borrowing and to the use
of the proceeds of these loans for the purchase of the goods
of American producers. In addition to business from abroad
there were in the United States itself two factors which stimulated industry: the enormous increase in the volume of construction, first making up the shortage in building occasioned
by war-time conditions, later on developing into a vast speculative boom; and the swift growth of new industries whose
development involved not only the current production of automobiles, petroleum, electrical equipment, etc., but also the
construction of factories, industrial machinery, and roads. In
both instances the abnormal expansion in the volume of con-
sumers' credit, incurred for the purchase of mortgages and
houses and for the new products of industry, created an unstable and impermanent source of purchasing power and of
capital funds. This rough outline of the sources of the prosperity which prevailed from 1922 until 1929 suffices to indicate
their temporary and unstable character.

But even in those golden post-war years all the glitter was

not gold. The new industries were built up and partly operated by cheap immigrant labour, which in its unproductive years (immaturity) had not formed a burden for the American taxpayer. Moreover, those industries were not hampered by radical social legislation and, urged principally by the desire and necessity for adjustment in cost, constantly sought sources of cheaper labour and moved from one area to another. This meant that industry could support only a small American "labour bourgeoisie" as upholders of the "American standards of living." The famous principle of "high wages and low costs as a policy of enlightened industrial practice" found application only on a limited scale. The average number of unemployed was about 2,500,000 in the days of high prosperity. Agriculture was depressed; so were the cotton manufacture and coal industries. All these circumstances restricted not the desire but the purchasing power of the masses of the people.

Therefore it is not surprising that, even during the "new era" of the lush twenties, the productive capacity of the nation was not utilized to its fullest extent. The facts show that America actually produced more in 1929, for instance, than was consumed, and that it might readily have produced—with the existing resources, plant and equipment, and labour supply, and without improvement in methods—approximately 20 per cent more than it did produce. That was before the depression which increased the number of unemployed to over 10,000,000.

This potential capacity of the existing industry in connexion with increased man-hour efficiency and further introduction of labour-saving devices makes it highly improbable that southern agricultural labour can be absorbed after it is freed from the cotton fields. The tide of migration towards the cities, mentioned in the fourth chapter, has already turned. Although the rural farm population was smaller by at least 1,200,000 in

1930 than in 1920, the 1930 returns showed that in every state during the previous year about twice as many persons came to the farm from the city as left it for the city. The number of persons leaving farms in 1930 was the smallest in several years, and the number moving to farms was by far the largest. The result was that the farm population not only kept all of its excess of births over deaths (amounting to 399,000) but also gained 39,000 from the farm-city interchange, making the total increase in farm population 438,000. This condition was further accentuated in 1931, the excess of births over deaths being 441,000 and the excess of arrivals on farms over departures for cities rising rapidly to 207,000, making the increase in farm population 648,000. These urban *émigrés* have tended to develop subsistence farming on a low standard of living.

This natural trend is an important phenomenon.

Since industry will not provide the outlet for the unemployed agricultural labour in the South, the solution of its problems must be sought in the rural South itself. That solution cannot be anything less than the development of a free peasant economy. The vital interests of white and black are here at stake. It will be difficult to accomplish this end. It is not enough to provide credit and tell people to go ahead. The people are so accustomed to dependency and improvidence that they cannot at once stand by themselves. Furthermore, although agriculture, dairying, and stock raising can give them a certain amount of self-sufficiency, they need money as well. For certain groups it will be possible to find partial employment in forest preservation and lumbering, or in the new industries which are expected to arise in connexion with the Tennessee Valley Authority. However, systematic effort must be made to free the South from its "colonial economy," its dependence upon the Middle West for feed and food.

Planning and education are needed. Ancient ideals and slogans, such as "A free college education for everybody," should be abandoned, whereas conscious endeavours should be made to form a free peasant class. The school curriculum should be based on and adapted to the rural needs, not framed after an urban model. Here is a great task for the agricultural teachers under the direction of the state departments. Since this planning cannot be restricted to state lines, regular contact between men of vision in the different states should be established. As in the past when new ideas were introduced and new organizational forms had to be created, philanthropic foundations might take the initiative and the lead. Public opinion must be educated to understand the great issues. Although the interests of black and white are equally concerned, the peculiar situation of the South makes it necessary that, until these ideas are generally accepted, Negro interests have special attention. There should be organized contact between the state agents for Negro schools. Perhaps it will even be necessary to institute a liaison officer for the purpose of safeguarding effective co-operation.

For anyone who studies southern problems objectively, it is evident that there is an identity of black and white interests. Up until now the plantation legend has impeded the realization of this fact. Will it be otherwise in the future?

In our view of bi-racial situations in America we found prejudice everywhere, prejudice against aliens, the "new immigration," the Chinese, the Japanese, the Mexicans, and the Indians; but all these race relations were in flux. The immigrants move from their colonies to zones of second and third settlement, and gradually lose their marks of identity. Submerged classes of immigrants are replaced by others, and move one step higher up the social ladder. The bitter and bloody antagonism between Indians and whites has subsided: intermarriage effaces the differences. With the Spanish-speaking Americans the tendency is also towards conformity. As education progresses and the economic conditions of the various races improve, contrasts will be weakened. In the case of the American-born Chinese and Japanese, intermarriage with Italians, Mexicans, and others will increase as the lines between the colonies disappear.

However, for the Negro we found a petrification of relationships. In the cities of the North miscegenation takes place and cannot avoid weakening social barriers; but in the South, although much blood mixture is still going on, there is still no promise of a radical change in public opinion.

The South has now to make a choice. During the agricultural period of America (1830–70) the South experienced its Golden Age. Political leadership was with the South, but economically it depended on the North. The plantations were often run with the aid of northern capital, the factors in Savannah and Charleston being agents of northern financiers. Although the South produced the raw material which went to England and the North, it had to buy the finished product. As the South surrendered itself more and more exclusively to King Cotton, it became more and more dependent on the North for its feed and food supply.

This tendency towards a "colonial economy" was enhanced after the Civil War. Again the North provided the capital for economic reconstruction and forced the South, even to a larger extent, into cotton culture. What diversification existed was abandoned. After 1880, industry in the South developed rapidly. Textile mills, steel plants, coal mines, and turpentine and lumber industries grew, but again it was northern capital which sought this area of cheap labour and rich natural resources for gainful exploitation. Promoters of the "New South" of those days were the agents who encouraged a still greater dependency. Now the glory of King Cotton is vanishing. Will the "colony" that is the South follow the example of so many colonial possessions which have known an era of glamour when their products dominated European markets but have since fallen into oblivion? That state of oblivion will not easily be reached by the South because in its destitution and despondency it will devote itself entirely to the Negro problem. The lack of economic possibilities will be reflected in racial conflicts and increased criminality of which the world will be only too much aware.

Or will the rebel yell ring again, now sounding the voice of a real New South and expressing the determination to live its own life, build up its own economy, its own democracy of free, self-confident, self-sufficient citizens?

America, and particularly the South, offers a unique opportunity for the development of the new peasant. He will do as the old peasant did, produce his own food and the feed for his stock. With his fruit, maple syrup, cream and butter, home-cured hams, cereals, and vegetables, he will provide himself a healthier and more abundant diet than he has ever known. At the same time, in this age of radios, automobiles, movies, and telephones, he will not be isolated as was the pioneer. The word "peasant" brings unfavourable associations to the American mind. It suggests feudalism. The agriculturist wishes to be called a "farmer," but farming implies the production of commercial crops. However, the peasant is not a serf; he is a hard-working stubborn character, proud of his freedom and independence on his self-owned land.

In parts of America other than the South there are already indications of the evolution of a new rural life. A larger and more modern rural community is emerging, consisting of the village or town as its centre and the open country as its tributary territory. Now it is up to the South to choose. Once there was a time when people could allow themselves the luxury of disregarding the rural needs, when urbanization seemed to be the cure for all ills. But a new era has come, here as elsewhere. Now the only choice is between hopeless decay and a hopeful revival of rural life.

As the basis of a New South, the building up of a peasant economy is as vital to the whites as it is to the blacks and requires the co-operation of all. Intelligent planning and assiduous application of all available energy are needed. Will this be feasible? At present, Negro-white relationships are in a state of petrification. Will it be possible to break the spell of the plantation legend?

Note on Filipino Immigration

FILIPINO immigration gained strength after 1924. As early as May 1927 the first bill for exclusion of the Filipinos was introduced into Congress. In the same year and in 1928 the annual convention of the American Federation of Labor urged Congress to enact legislation. With the disturbances and race riots of the autumn of 1928, the question really entered national politics. Since the depression, residents of the regions in which Filipinos were thickly congregated could easily charge the latter with creating an unemployment situation and with lowering wages. The transitional status of the Philippine Islands—now definitely assured of complete independence—has opened the possibility of putting Filipino immigration as well as Filipino sugar under quota. A recent act empowers the government to send unemployed Filipinos back to their native country. The Filipino incident on the Pacific Coast is closed.

The difficulties which Filipino immigrants had to face in America differed from those of the Japanese and the Chinese mainly in this respect: before entering the continent these Filipinos had already enjoyed American administration and education, and had imbibed the American ideals of freedom and equality which are not in accordance with the "place" racial discrimination allowed them. Moreover, although not citizens, they were not "immigrants" because they were not "aliens," for they owed no allegiance to any foreign government.

The anti-Filipino movement had primarily an economic basis. Not only on the ranches but also elsewhere they were competitors. They displaced Americans as elevator operators and bell boys, waiters, hotel attendants, Pullman porters, and seamen in coastwise shipping. That is the reason why Mexicans and Negroes also joined the anti-Filipino movement. On the other hand they aroused the slumbering California anti-Oriental sentiment by their relationships with white girls. Practically all these Filipinos were young men under thirty-five. Freed from the social restraints imposed by the native community in the Islands, far from home, lonesome, unadjusted, and lacking wholesome recreation, they sought female companionship and courtship, but thereby hurt the ingrained feelings of the Coast. Lynching and mobbing were the result.

Bibliography

NOTE: The books and articles listed here are not intended as anything like a complete bibliography of these large subjects. They are rather the principal reference works which the author consulted and upon which he relied for correcting and amplifying his observations and impressions. No bibliography is given for Chapter VI, since many of the important works on this topic are referred to in the text or given in the bibliography of other chapters.

I: THE CHINESE IN CALIFORNIA

Coolidge, Mary Elizabeth Burrough (Roberts) Smith, *Chinese Immigration* (1909).

Cross, Ira B., *A History of the Labor Movement in California* (University of California Publications in Economics, vol. 14; 1935).

Eaves, Lucile, *A History of California Labor Legislation* (University of California Publications in Economics, vol. 2; 1910).

Liu, Chiang, "Chinese versus American Ideas Concerning the Family" (*Journal of Applied Sociology*, vol. 10, p. 41).

Louis, Kit King, "Problems of Second Generation Chinese" (*Sociology and Social Research*, vol. 16, p. 250).

Louis, Kit King, *A Study of American-Born and American-Reared Chinese in Los Angeles* (Master's thesis, University of Southern California, 1931).

McKenzie, R. D., *Oriental Exclusion* (1928).

Mears, Eliot Grinnell, *Resident Orientals on the American Pacific Coast, Their Legal and Economic Status* (1928).

Renner, George T., "Chinese Influence in the Development of Western United States" (*The Annals of the American Academy of Political and Social Science*, vol. 152, p. 356).

Reynolds, Charles Nathan, "Oriental-White Race Relations in Santa Clara County, California" (Dissertation, Stanford University, 1926–27; *Stanford University Bulletin*, 5th series, no. 47, vol. 2, p. 182).

Seward, George F., *Chinese Immigration in its Social and Economic Aspects* (1881).

Smith, W. C., "Changing Personality Traits of Second Generation Orientals in America" (*American Journal of Sociology*, vol. 33, pp. 922–9).

Smith, W. C., "The Second Generation Oriental-American" (*Journal of Applied Sociology*, vol. 10, p. 160).

Sterry, Nora, "Social Attitudes of Chinese Immigrants" (*Journal of Applied Sociology*, vol. 7, p. 325).

NOTE: Professor E. S. Bogardus permitted consultation of certain recent research studies made by students in his department, the School of Social Welfare, at the University of Southern California. I have not separately listed under this and subsequent sections the various journal papers of Dr. Bogardus which I found very helpful.

II: THE JAPANESE IN CALIFORNIA

Buell, Raymond Leslie, "The Development of the Anti-Japanese Agitation in the United States" (*Political Science Quarterly*, December 1922; December 1923).

Buell, Raymond Leslie, "Japanese Immigration" (*World Peace Foundation Pamphlet*, vol. 7, nos. 5 and 6; 1924).

Darsie, M. J., "The American-Born Japanese" (*Sociology and Social Research*, vol. 19, p. 161).

Garis, Roy L., *Immigration Restriction* (1927).

Ichihashi, Yamamoto, *Japanese in the United States* (1932).

Kataoka, W. T., "Occupations of Japanese in Los Angeles" (*Sociology and Social Research*, vol. 14, p. 53).

Michinari, Fujita, "Japanese Associations in America" (*Sociology and Social Research*, vol. 13, p. 211).

Miller, H. A., *The Japanese Problem in the United States* (1915).

Pritchard, Earl H., "The Japanese Exclusion Bill of 1924" (*Research Studies of the State College of Washington*, vol. 2, no. 2; May 1930).

Strong, Edward K., Jr., *Japanese in California* (1933).

Strong, Edward K., Jr., *The Second-Generation Japanese Problem* (1933).

Svensrud, Marian, "Attitudes of the Japanese toward their Language Schools" (*Sociology and Social Research*, vol. 17, p. 259).

Tsutomu, Obana, "The Changing Japanese Situation in California" (*Pacific Affairs*, vol. 5; 1932).

III: MEXICANS AND INDIANS

MEXICANS

Albig, William, "Opinions Concerning Mexican Immigrants" (*Sociology and Social Research*, vol. 15, p. 62).

Allen, Ruth A., "Mexican Peon Women in Texas" (*Sociology and Social Research*, vol. 16, p. 131).

Bogardus, Emory S., *The Mexican in the United States* (1934).

Gamio, Manuel, *Mexican Immigration to the United States* (1930).

Gamio, Manuel, *The Mexican Immigrant* (1931).

Handman, M. S., "Economic Reasons for the Coming of the Mexican Immigrant" (*American Journal of Sociology*, vol. 35, p. 601).

Manuel, Herschel T., *The Education of Mexican and Spanish-Speaking Children in Texas* (1930).

Manuel, Herschel T., "The Mexican Population of Texas," (*Southwestern Social Science Quarterly*, vol. 15, pp. 29–51).

Santiago, Hasel D., "Mexican Influences in Southern California" (*Sociology and Social Research*, vol. 16, p. 68).

Taylor, Paul S., "Mexican Labor in the United States" (*University of California Publications in Economics*, vols. 6, 7, 12, 13).

Walker, Helen W., "Mexican Immigrants as Laborers" (*Sociology and Social Research*, vol. 13, p. 55).

INDIANS

Blackmar, Frank W., "American Indian and Status" (*Sociology and Social Research*, vol. 14, p. 221).

Blackmar, Frank W., "The Socialization of the American Indian" (*American Journal of Sociology*, vol. 34, p. 653).

Blackmar, Frank W., *Spanish Institutions of the Southwest* (1891).

Jackson, Helen, *A Century of Dishonor* (1903).

Macleod, William Christie, *The American Indian Frontier* (1928).

Macleod, William Christie, "Big Business and the North American Indian" (*American Journal of Sociology*, vol. 34, p. 480).

Mead, Margaret, *The Changing Culture of an Indian Tribe* (1932).

Meriam, Lewis, *The Problem of Indian Administration* (1928).

Radin, Paul, *The Story of the American Indian* (1927).

Reichard, Gladys A., *Social Life of the Navajo Indians* (1928).

Schmeckebier, Lawrence F., *The Office of Indian Affairs* (1927).

IV: AMERICA AND THE ALIEN

Bogardus, Emory S., *Immigration and Race Attitudes* (1928).

Burgess, Ernest W., *The Urban Community* (1926).

Daniels, John, *America Via the Neighborhood* (1920).

Drachsler, Julius, *Democracy and Assimilation* (1920).

Fairchild, Henry Pratt, *The Melting-Pot Mistake* (1926).

Jerome, Harry, *Migration and Business Cycles* (1926).

Lasker, Bruno, *Jewish Experiences in America* (1930).

Lynd, Robert S., and Lynd, Helen Merrill, *Middletown* (1929).

Mayo, Elton, *The Human Problems of an Industrial Civilization* (1933).

McCormick, Thomas C., "Major Trends in Rural Life in the United States" (*American Journal of Sociology*, vol. 36; March 1931).

Miller, H. A., *Race, Nations and Classes* (1924).

Niebuhr, H. Richard, *The Social Sources of Denominationalism* (1929).

Page, Kirby, *Recent Gains in American Civilization* (1928).

Park, Robert E., Burgess, Ernest W., and McKenzie, Roderick D., *The City* (1925).

Park, Robert E., and Miller, Herbert A., *Old World Traits Transplanted* (1925).

Parrington, Vernon L., *Main Currents in American Thought* (1927).

Recent Economic Changes in the United States (Report of the Committee on Recent Economic Changes of the President's Conference on Unemployment, 2 vols.; 1929).

Recent Social Trends in the United States (Report of the President's Research Committee of Social Trends, 2 vols.; 1933).

Ross, Edward Alsworth, *The Old World in the New* (1914).

Shaw, Clifford R., *Delinquency Areas* (1929).

Thomas, W. I., and Znaniecki, Florian, *The Polish Peasant in Europe and America* (1918–20).

Thrasher, Frederick M., *The Gang* (1927).

Wirth, Louis, *The Ghetto* (1928).

Young, Donald, *American Minority Peoples* (1932).

Young, Donald, "The Modern American Family" (*The Annals of the American Academy of Political and Social Science*, vol. 160; March 1932).

Zorbaugh, Harvey Warren, *The Gold Coast and the Slum* (1929).

V: THE SOUTH AND THE NEGRO

Ball, William Watts, *The State That Forgot* (1932).

Bowen, Trevor, *Divine White Right* (1934).

Bowers, Claude G., *The Tragic Era* (1929).

Brawley, Benjamin G., *A Social History of the American Negro* (1921).

Couch, William T., *Culture in the South* (1934).

Cutler, James Elbert, *Lynch Law* (1905).

Den Hollander, Dr. A. N. F., *De landelijke arme blanken in het Zuiden der Vereenigde Staten* (1933).

Dodd, William E., *The Cotton Kingdom* (1919).

Dowd, Jerome, *The Negro in American Life* (1926).

Du Bois, W. E. Burghardt, *Black Reconstruction* (1935).

Du Bois, W. E. Burghardt, *The Gift of Black Folk* (1924).

Du Bois, W. E. Burghardt, *The Souls of Black Folk* (1903).

Edwards, Paul K., *The Southern Urban Negro as a Consumer* (1932).

Embree, Edwin R., *Brown America* (1931).

Frazier, E. Franklin, *The Negro Family in Chicago* (1932).

Gaines, Francis Pendleton, *The Southern Plantation* (1924).

Gosnell, Harold F., *Negro Politicians: The Rise of Negro Politics in Chicago* (1935).

I'll Take My Stand, written by twelve Southerners (1930).

Johnson, Charles S., *The Negro in American Civilization* (1930).

Johnson, Charles S., *Shadow of the Plantation* (1934).

Knight, Edgar W., *Education in the South* (1924).

Lewinson, Paul, *Race, Class, and Party* (1932).

Lynch, John R., *The Facts of Reconstruction* (1913).

McCord, Charles H., *The American Negro* (1914).

Mecklin, John Moffatt, *The Ku Klux Klan* (1924).

Mims, Edwin, *The Advancing South* (1926).

Moton, Robert Russa, *What the Negro Thinks* (1929).

Odum, Howard W., *An American Epoch* (1930).

Phillips, Ulrich Bonnell, *American Negro Slavery* (1927).

Phillips, Ulrich Bonnell, *Life and Labor in the Old South* (1929).

Raper, Arthur,[1] *The Tragedy of Lynching* (1933).

Reuter, Edward, *The American Race Problem* (1927).

Skaggs, William H., *The Southern Oligarchy* (1924).

Spero, Sterling D., and Harris, Abram L., *The Black Worker* (1931).

Stowe, Harriet Beecher, *Uncle Tom's Cabin* (1881).

Thomas, William Hannibal, *The American Negro* (1901).

Vance, Rupert B., *Human Factors in Cotton Culture* (1929).

Vance, Rupert B., *Human Geography of the South* (1932, 1935).

Washington, Booker T., *Up from Slavery* (1900).

Weatherford, Willis D., and Johnson, Charles S., *Race Relations* (1934).

Wesley, Charles H., *Negro Labor in the United States* (1927).

Woodson, Carter G., *The Rural Negro* (1930).

Woodson, Carter G., and Greene, Lorenzo J., *The Negro Wage Earner* (1930).

Young, Donald, "The American Negro" (*The Annals of the American Academy of Political and Social Science*, vol. 140; November 1928).

[1] Dr. Raper also permitted consultation of his unprinted Ph.D. dissertation (University of North Carolina, 1931), an intensive study of "Two Black Belt Counties" in Georgia.

VII: PREJUDICE OR PROGRESS [1]

Black, John D., "Agricultural Planning and Control" (*Journal of Farm Economics*, vol. 17, no. 1; February 1935).

Black, John D., "The Outlook for American Cotton" (*Review of Economic Statistics*; March 15, 1935).

De Wilde, John C., "The AAA and Exports of the South" (*Foreign Policy Reports*; April 24, 1935).

Gard, Wayne, and Thomas, Norman, "Decline in the Cotton Kingdom" (*Current History*; April 1935).

Johnson, Charles S., Embree, Edwin R., and Alexander, W. W., *The Collapse of Cotton Tenancy* (1935).

Leven, Maurice, Moulton, Harold G., and Warburton, Clark, *America's Capacity to Consume* (1934).

Nourse, Edwin G., and Associates, *America's Capacity to Produce* (1934).

Vance, Rupert B., *Regional Reconstruction: A Way Out for the South* (1935).

Zimmerman, C. C., "Discussion of Subsistence Homesteads" (*Journal of Farm Economics*, vol. 16, no. 1; January 1934).

Zimmerman, Erich W., "Resources of the South" (*The South Atlantic Quarterly*, vol. 32, no. 3; July 1933).

APPENDIX: NOTE ON FILIPINO IMMIGRATION

Anthony, Donald E., "Filipino Labor in Central California" (*Sociology and Social Research*, vol. 16, p. 149).

Foster, Nellie, "Legal Status of Filipino Intermarriages" (*Sociology and Social Research*, vol. 16, p. 441).

Gonsalo, D. F., "Social Adjustments of Filipinos in America" (*Sociology and Social Research*, vol. 14, p. 166).

Lasker, Bruno, *Filipino Immigration* (1931).

[1] Literature quoted at the head of previous chapters is not repeated here. See also the Introduction.

Index